# The Syndicated
# News Articles

# Books by Eric Hoffer

The True Believer

The Passionate State of Mind

The Ordeal of Change

The Temper of Our Time

Working and Thinking on the Waterfront

First Things, Last Things

Reflections on the Human Condition

In Our Time

Before the Sabbath

Between the Devil and the Dragon

Truth Imagined

The Syndicated News Articles

# The Syndicated News Articles

## Eric Hoffer

Hopewell Publications

Published by Hopewell
Publications, LLC
PO Box 11, Titusville, NJ
08560-0011 (609) 818-1049

**info@HopePubs.com**
**www.HopePubs.com**

International Standard Book Number: 9781933435374

Library of Congress Control Number: 2011935178

First Edition

Printed in the United States of America

Thanks to the Eric Hoffer Project (www.HofferProject.org)
for archival assistance in assembling this book.

Photographs taken from the Hoffer estate private archives.

Author photo courtesy of
The Bancroft Library, University of California, Berkeley.

*To the memory of Lili Fabilli Osborne,
whose lifelong love and dedication
helped keep Eric Hoffer's words alive
and in the hearts of contemporary thinkers.*

———————————————

*I speak the truth, not so much as I would,
but as much as I dare;
and I dare a little more, as I grow older.*

- Michel de Montaigne

If anybody asks me what I have accomplished, I will say all I have accomplished is that I have written a few good sentences.

—Eric Hoffer

# Table of Contents

# Table of Contents

# Table of Contents

# Table of Contents

# Foreword

From 1968 to 1970, Eric Hoffer, the popular "longshoreman philosopher" wrote a weekly news column that appeared in approximately 200 papers across the United States. The articles were terse, tour de force essays, offered to the public with no apology and the conviction of a great thinker. The topics discussed were always of a social nature and the mechanics of human behavior. Hoffer fearlessly delved into the issues of the day, and reaped a full spectrum of public reaction, which he handled with dignity, humor, and humility. It is clear that he sought not only an understanding of but also a solution to contemporary problems. Sixty years later, many of these insights still hold true.

The columns in this collection are presented in chronological order and were titled for archival purposes. They were originally submitted without titles, since it is common practice for newspaper editors to create headlines with respect to the perceived sensibilities of a newspaper's readership. Hoffer painstakingly scripted every word and insisted that his prose never be altered, although the request was not always respected. This collection restores his original prose. Certain phrases seem dated, employing terms such as "Negro" for African American or "Orient" for the eastern regions of the globe. In this emotionally and politically sensitive world, it would humor Hoffer that these precise words offend anyone.

The impact of his words continually surprised and fascinated Hoffer. In 1951, the publication of his first book spurred a public discourse that continues until this day. *The True Believer* both coined the often-used phrase and sealed his reputation as a voice to be heeded, even though Hoffer, along with many of his associates, believed that his second book, *The Ordeal of Change*, was his finest work. Hoffer was perhaps one of the most prolific readers in history, consuming volumes of reference and literature to achieve his searing perspectives on humanity. In the end, he would write nine original books and countless articles.

The syndicated news columns ran at the height of Hoffer's popularity. This was not long after he gave a series of television interviews with journalist Eric Sevareid that greatly expanded interest in his work. Hoffer's opinions became more bold and his writing more artful, developing the concepts of man, nature, and the human connection to God and the devil. During this period, Hoffer became committed to lectures and other engagements, and eventually felt the strain of a weekly news deadline. When he withdrew from public life, he spent his days in a quiet ritual of journaling and summits with friends and the occasional dignitary or intellectual who visited his San Francisco home. Hoffer gave no more interviews and no more lectures. When the last article in this collection was penned in April 1970, he promised to "crawl back in my hole, where I started." The process of withdrawal was under-way. He feared that he had become somewhat of a "public scold," which ran counter to his broad-thinking and gregarious, welcoming personality.

This collection provides the sketch of a man who resisted popular fashion in favor of a deeper understanding of the human condition. Reaching across time, Hoffer gathered a portrait of humanity: the very essence of separating our spirit from the flesh and the duality that exists between the two. In many ways, Hoffer's work remains relevant because year by year and decade by decade we remain as human as ever.

Christopher Klim
February 2011

*Christopher Klim, archival editor of this collection, is a novelist and journalist who has successfully led a decade-long effort to restore Eric Hoffer's works to print.*

# The Disenfranchised Can Shape Us

## January 14, 1968

There is in us a tendency to judge a race, a nation, or an organization by its least worthy members. The tendency is manifestly perverse and unfair, yet it has some justification. For the quality and destiny of a nation are determined to a considerable extent by the nature and potentialities of its inferior elements.

The inert mass of a nation is its middle section. The industrious, decent, well-to-do, and satisfied middle classes whether in cities or on the land are worked upon and shaped by minorities at both extremes: the best and the worst.

The superior individual, whether in politics, business, industry, science, literature or religion, undoubtedly plays a major role in the shaping of a nation. But so do the individuals at the other extreme: the poor, the outcasts, the misfits, and those who are in the grip of some overpowering passion.

The importance of these inferior elements as formative factors lies in the readiness with which they are swayed in any direction. This peculiarity is due to their inclination to take risks ("not giving a damn") and their propensity for united action. They crave to merge their drab, wasted lives into something grand and complete.

Thus they are the first and most fervent adherents of new religions, political upheavals, patriotic hysteria, gangs, and mass rushes to new lands.

And the quality of a nation—its innermost worth—is made manifest by its dregs as they rise to the top; by how brave they are, how humane, how skilled, how generous, how independent or servile, by the bounds they will not transgress in their dealings with man's soul, with truth, and with honor.

The average American of today bristles with indignation when he is told that this country was built, largely by hordes of undesirables from Europe. Yet, far from being derogatory, this statement, if true, should be a cause for rejoicing, should fortify our pride in the stock from which we have sprung.

This vast continent with its towns, farms, factories, dams, aqueducts, docks, railroads, highways, powerhouses, schools, and parks is the handwork of common folk from the Old World, where for centuries men of their kind had been beasts of burden, the property of their masters—kings, nobles, and priests—and with no will and no aspirations of their own. When on rare occasions one of the lowly had reached the top in Europe he had kept the pattern intact and, if anything, tightened the screws.

The stuffy little corporal[1] from Corsica harnessed the lusty forces released by the French Revolution to a gilded state coach, and could think of nothing grander than mixing his blood with that of the Hapsburg masters and establishing a new dynasty. In our day a bricklayer[2] in Italy, a house painter[3] in Germany, and a shoemaker's son[4] in Russia have made themselves masters of their nations, and what they did was to re-establish and reinforce the old pattern.

Only here, in America, were the common folk of the Old World given a chance to show what they could do on their own, without a master to push and order them about.

History contrived an earthshaking joke when it lifted by the nape of the neck lowly peasants, shopkeepers, laborers, paupers,

---

[1] Napoleon Bonaparte (1769-1821), French Emperor.
[2] Benito Mussolini (1883-1945), Italian leader of the Fascist Party.
[3] Adolph Hitler (1889-1945), German leader of the Nazi Party.
[4] Joseph Stalin (1878-1953), Russian leader of the Soviet Union.

jailbirds, and drunks from the midst of Europe, dumped them on a vast, virgin continent and said, "Go to it, it is yours!"

And the lowly were not awed by the magnitude of the task. A hunger for action, pent up for centuries, found an outlet. They went to it with ax, pick, shovel, plow, and rifle; on foot, on horse, in wagons, and on flatboats. They went to it praying, howling, singing, brawling, drinking, and fighting. Make way for the people! This is how I read the statement that this country was built by hordes of undesirables from the Old World.

Small wonder that we in this country have a deeply ingrained faith in human regeneration. We believe that, given a chance, even the degraded and the apparently worthless are capable of constructive work and great deeds. It is a faith founded on experience, not on some idealistic theory.

And no matter what some anthropologists, sociologists, and geneticists may tell us, we shall go on believing that man, unlike other forms of life, is not a captive of his past—of his heredity and habits—but is possessed of infinite plasticity, and his potentialities for good and for evil are never wholly exhausted.

# Minority Pride Required for Change

January 21, 1968

The plight of the Negro in America is that he is a Negro first and only secondly an individual. Only when the Negro community as a whole performs something that will win for it the admiration of the world will the Negro individual be completely himself.

Another way of putting it is that the Negro in America needs pride in his people, their achievements, their leaders—before he can attain self-respect. At present, individual achievement cannot cure the Negro's soul. No matter how manifest his superiority as an individual, he cannot savor "the unbought grace of life."

The predicament of the Negro in America, then, is that what he needs most is something he cannot give himself; something moreover, which neither governments, nor legislators, nor courts, but only the Negro community as a whole can give him.

Despite the vehement protestations of Negro writers and intellectuals, the Negro is not the white man's problem. On the contrary, the white man is the Negro's chief problem. As things are now, the Negro is what the white man says he is—he knows himself only by white hearsay.

That which corrodes the soul of the Negro is his monstrous inner agreement with the prevailing prejudice against him. To annul the white hearsay and be what he chooses to be, the Negro must become his own playwright, stage his own play, and cast himself in a role of his own choosing.

The Negro needs genuine, unequivocal heroes. Martyrs or slogan-slingers cannot make history. Surely, if in Israel a few thousand fugitives from gas chambers stood up on their hind legs and defied forty million Arabs, it should he possible for American Negroes to stand up to a pack of cowardly white trash. The black counties in Alabama and Mississippi are more truly the homeland of the Negro than Palestine is the homeland of the Jew.

Yet one has the impression that the Negro has no taste for the patient, quiet organizational work which is the taproot of any durable social achievement. The prevailing feeling seems to be that everything the Negro needs must come full grown from without.

When James Baldwin[5] went to Israel several years ago there was something in him that kept him from seeing what he should have seen, namely, a paradigm of what the weak can do to heal their souls. He wrote instead an article for *Harper's* magazine in which he said that a cynical Britain and a cynical America gave Palestine to the Jews.

To Baldwin it is self-evident that if you have something it is because someone gave it to you.

One begins to wonder whether the American Negro has the capacity to create a genuine community with organs for cooperation and self-help. You strain your ears in vain amid the present Negro clamor for a small voice saying: "Leave us alone and we will show you what we can do." If it be true that the only effective way to help the Negro is to help him help himself, then the Negro's aversion to, or perhaps incapacity for, a self-starting, do-it-yourself way of life makes it questionable whether he can ever attain freedom and self-respect.

One cannot think of another instance where a minority striving for equality has been so deficient in the capacity for mutual aid and cooperation. Almost invariably when a Negro makes his mark in whatever walk of life his impulse is to escape the way of life, the mores and the atmosphere of the Negro people.

The well-off or educated Negro may use his fellow Negroes to enrich himself (insurance, newspaper publishing, cosmetics) or to advance his career in the professions or in politics, but he will not lift a finger to lighten the burden of his people. Thus, the most enterprising and ambitious segment of the Negro population has segregated itself from the Negro millions who are left to wallow in the cesspools of frustration which are the Negro ghettos.

---

[5] James Baldwin (1924-1987), American writer and civil rights activist.

# Automation Key to Man's Ascension

**January 28, 1968**

When God created the world He immediately automated it, and there was nothing left for Him to do. So in His boredom He began to tinker and experiment. Man was a runaway experiment.

It was in a mood of divine recklessness that God created man. "In the image of God created He him," and it was a foregone conclusion that a creature this made would try to emulate and surpass his creator.

And, indeed, no sooner did God create man than He was filled with misgivings and suspicions. He could not take His eyes of His last and strangest creation. I can see Jehovah leaning over a bank of clouds contemplating the strange creature as it puttered about under the trees in the garden of Eden, wondering what was going on in the creature's head—what thoughts, what dreams, what plans and what plots.

The early chapters of Genesis make it plain that God was worried and took no chances. The moment man ate from the tree of knowledge God had His worst fears confirmed. He drove man out of Eden and cursed him for good measure.

But you do not stop a conspirator by exiling him. I can see Adam get up from the dust after he had been bounced out, shake his fist at the closed gates of Eden and the watching angels, and mutter: "I will return."

Though condemned to wrestle with a cursed earth for his bread and fight off thistles and thorns, man resolved in the depths of his soul to become indeed a creator—to create a manmade world that would straddle and tame God's creation.

Thus all through the millennia of man's existence the vying with God has been a leading motif of his strivings and efforts. Much of the time of the motif, is drowned by the counterpoint of everyday life, but it is clear and unmistakable in times of great venturesomeness.

It was the machine age that really launched the manmade creation. The machine was man's way of breathing will and thought into inanimate matter. Unfortunately, the second creation did not quite come off.

Unlike God, man could not immediately automate his manmade world. He was not inventive enough. Until yesterday, the machine remained a half-machine; it lacked the gears and filaments of will and thought, and man had to use his fellow men as a stopgap for inventiveness. He had to yoke men, women and children with iron and steam.

★

There was no escape for the mass of people from the ravenous maws of factories and mines. If they crossed the ocean and came to America the factories and mines were there waiting to receive them.

Then yesterday, almost unnoticed, the automated machine edged onto the stage. It was born in the laboratories of technical schools where mathematicians and engineers were trying to duplicate the human brain.

And it was brought into the factory not to cure the disease of work which has tortured humanity for untold generations, but to eliminate man from the productive process.

Power is always charged with the impulse to eliminate human nature, the human variable, from the equation of action. Dictators do it by terror or by the inculcation of blind faith, the military does it by iron discipline, and the industrial masters think they can do it by automation.

But the world has not fallen into the hands of commissars, generals and the National Association of Manufacturers. There is a change of climate now taking place everywhere which is unfavorable to the exercise of absolute power. Even in totalitarian countries the demands of common folk are becoming factors in economic, social, and political decisions.

There is, therefore, a chance that the denouement of automation might be what we want it to be.

# When the Intellectuals Take Charge

## February 4, 1968

The cold war between the intellectual and the middle class which raged through the 19$^{th}$ century came to a head in the 20th, and it now seems to be culminating in the triumph of the intellectuals.

The priests and chaplains who are stirring up riots, the theorists who propose to better the condition of the people by stripping them of their earnings through increased taxation, and the educators who want to herd two-year olds into classrooms so as to control their first infantile thought, are among the intellectuals who today wage a cold war on America.

In the same way, under one guise or another, in many parts of the world, the middle class is being stripped of power and treasure and is trampled underfoot, not by proletarians or aristocrats, but by self-styled intellectuals. Napoleon saw it coming. "Cannon," he said, "killed the feudal system, ink will kill the modem social organization." In many parts of the world there are now intellectuals acting as large-scale industrialists, as military leaders, as statesmen and empire builders.

By intellectual I mean a literate person who feels himself a member of the educated minority. It is not actual intellectual superiority which makes the intellectual but the feeling of belonging to an intellectual class. Indeed, the less valid his claim to intellectual superiority the more typical will be the intellectual.

In Asia, Africa and Latin America, every student, every petty member of the professions, and every clerk feels himself equipped for national leadership. In Britain and Western Europe the intellectual, though not as assertive in claiming his birthright to direct and order society, nevertheless feels far superior to the practical men of action, the traditional leaders in politics and business. In the Communist countries, the intelligentsia constitutes the ruling class.

Intellectual activity does not automatically yield an unequivocal sense of usefulness. Even so accomplished an intellectual as Tycho Brehe[6] groaned as he died, "Oh, that it may not seem that I have lived in vain." Hence the intellectual's need for a formal status—a degree, a title, membership in an elite—to bolster his confidence and self-esteem.

However much he battles for democracy, the intellectual is basically aristocratic, and feels at home in a hierarchical social order. He knows with every fibre of his being that men are not equal, and there are few things he cares for less than a classless society.

It is this vital need for an acknowledged status that renders the intellectual sensitive to social differences, and prompts him to see classes even where they are not clearly marked.

Power seems to corrupt the intellectual more than it does other human types. We find again and again that when the intellectual comes to power he is not satisfied with mere obedience but wants to reshape souls to his own specifications. The Catholic Church at the height of its power, and the Nazi and Communist dictatorships, are instances of intellectual hierarchies practicing the black art of soul raping. To some extent this was also true of the psycho-analytical movement. The prototype of the Communist confessions is to be found in Otto Rank's[7] abject recantation of his heretical tendencies after he was drawn into a series of analytical conferences with Freud.[8]

---

[6] Tycho Brehe (1546-1601), Danish astronomer, alchemist, and researcher.
[7] Otto Rank (1884-1939), Austrian psychoanalyst, writer, and teacher.
[8] Sigmund Freud (1856-1939), Austrian neurologist who founded psychoanalysis.

★

It is disconcerting that practical men of action—businessmen, engineers, politicians, soldiers—should, on the whole, be less corrupted by power than philosophers, artists, poets, scholars, and intellectuals in general. Seen thus, the moderateness and democracy of the Anglo Saxon nations in the past may be due to their tradition of keeping intellectuals away from power, and of not paying attention to their political views.

Intellectuals are likely to consider any achievement not fathered by words as illegitimate. Hence their disdain of things which have come to pass by chance. One of the reasons that America as it is is without appeal to the intellectual is that it does not manifest the realization of a grand design, and the solemn ritual of making the word become flesh. The masses eloped with history to America and have lived in a common-law marriage with it, unhallowed by ritual and the incantations of the intellectuals.

To the intellectual, America's unforgivable sin is that it has revolutions without revolutionaries, and achieves the momentous in a mater-of-fact way. The real shock will come when America achieves socialism without socialists.

# The Cauldron of Youth

**February 11, 1968**

Northwestern University in Evanston, Ill., has recently ended its annual student-organized symposium. The theme was "Violence in America," including political action, societal behavior and communication through the media and the arts, but the scheduled subjects were quickly sidetracked and all discussion centered on the issue of violence—including student violence—in the attainment of civil rights.

In rather recent months, newspapers have reported student riots in Spain, Iran, Turkey, India, South Vietnam, North Korea, Japan and Mexico—to mention but a few—in addition to the almost uncounted student disturbances in our own schools and universities.

One's first reaction is, "Juvenile delinquents trying to change the world," until we realize that history has always been made by men who have the restlessness, impressionability, credulity, capacity for make-believe, ruthlessness and self-righteousness of children, and that our process of higher education for big segments of our youth has kept these students children.

Until relatively recent times man's span of life was short. Throughout most of history the truly old were a rarity. In an excavation of one of the world's oldest cemeteries, the skeletons showed that the average age of the population at death was twenty-five, and there is no reason to suppose that the place was unusually unhealthy.

14

Thus it seems plausible that the momentous discoveries and inventions of the Neolithic Age[9]—the domestication of animals and plants, the invention of the wheel, sail and plough, the discovery of irrigation, fermentation and metallurgy—were the work of an almost childlike population, and were perhaps made in the course of play. Nor is it likely that the ancient myths and legends, with their fairy-tale pattern and erotic symbolism, were elaborated by burnt-out old men.

The history of less ancient periods, too, reveals the juvenile character of their chief actors. Many observers have remarked on the smallness of the armor which has come down to us from the Middle Ages. Actually the men who wore the armor were not grownups. They were married at thirteen, were warriors and leaders in their teens, and senile at thirty-five or forty.

Nor did things change markedly in the sixteenth century. Montaigne[10] tells us that he hardly ever met a man as old as 50. Salvador de Madariaga[11] says of Spain's great age (1550-1650) that in those days "boys of 15 were men; men of 40 were old men." He adds that when the dramatists of that age designated a man as old they meant a man of about 40—yellow-skinned, wrinkle-faced and toothless.

In our time one has to ask children and the ignorant for news of the future. The saying in the Talmud that after the destruction of the temple prophecy was taken from the wise and given to children and fools reflects the disarray and perplexity of a time of trouble. When things become unhinged wisdom and experience are a handicap in discerning the shape of things to come.

---

[9]  Neolithic Age (approx. 10000 to 3000 BC), referred to as the New Stone Age.
[10] Michel de Montaigne (1533-1592), French Renaissance essayist and philosopher whose work greatly influenced Eric Hoffer.
[11] Salvadore de Madariaga (1886-1978), Spanish diplomat, writer, and historian.

The ignorant are a reservoir of daring. It almost seems that they who have yet to discover the known are particularly equipped for dealing with the unknown. The unlearned have often rushed in where the learned feared to tread, and it is the credulous who are tempted to attempt the impossible. Where you see a revolution taking place without revolutionaries there the vulgar and the ignorant are at work. They know not whither they go, and give chance a chance.

Often in the past the wise were unaware of the great mutations which were unfolding before their eyes. How many of the learned knew in the early decades of the 19th century that they had an industrial revolution on their hands? The discovery of America hardly touched the learned, but it influenced the minds of common folk.

In the student disturbances, as in the Negro riots, there is an alliance between juveniles and an element—in this case Marxists and civil rightists—to whom the disturbances are a windfall. The majority of the students, intimidated—even physically—by slogan-singing two-bit idealists, remain voiceless; and since there is no voting they cannot make themselves heard nor their disapprobation felt.

# Minority Revolution is Rootless

## February 18, 1968

Whether it be legitimate or not to expect as much from the Negro as we expect from ourselves, it is clear that we can expect little from the Negro as long as he does not expect much from himself.

Just now it is being taken for granted that the average Negro is not competent to bring up his own children, build his own house, initiate undertakings in business or agriculture, build a community. He prefers self-pity to self-confidence, and wanton violence to sustained effort.

The Negro leaders seem to have little faith in the character and potentialities of the Negro masses. Their words and acts are largely directed toward non-Negro America. They are not aware of the Negro masses as a reservoir of power and as an instrument of destiny.

And this lack of faith in the Negro masses is dictating the singular pattern of the Negro revolution. Its objectives, tactics and finances are not predicated on massive Negro backing. A cursory check among my Negro fellow longshoremen on the San Francisco waterfront while I was still working there—some 2,000 of them earning between $7,000 and $10,000 a year—showed that not one of those questioned had been asked to contribute to the Negro cause and not one of them had come near a CORE[12] picket line, whereas many white longshoremen received requests for money

---

[12] Congress of Racial Equality (CORE), a U.S. civil rights organization founded in 1942 to seek an end to segregation through nonviolence.

from Negro organizations, and some of them, and their daughters, were passionately involved in CORE affairs.

Since the revolution has no root in the Negro masses, it cannot grow. It cannot engage in long-range programs which after a period of maturing may yield an abundance of striking results. It goes for immediate, showy objectives. It operates wholly in the present, and has no thought of the future.

In the past, wherever there were many wrongs to right, the one least capable of yielding palpable results was attacked first. In early 19th century England the abuses which called for remedy were many. There was unimaginable poverty among the masses, and a lack of protection by law of the weak, yet the attack which rallied all the reforming forces was directed against parliamentary corruption.

One has the feeling that the prospect of Negro equality would have been brighter had the first target been disfranchisement rather than segregation. But the Negro leaders, having no faith and no roots in the Negro masses, cannot wait for votes to yield results. They cannot heed Nkrumah's[13] advice: "Seek ye first the political kingdom and all others shall be added unto it."

The questionable nature of the Negro revolution manifests itself in its choice of enemies—real enemies are too dangerous—and the way to come by tame enemies is to declare that your friends, the white liberals, are enemies because they are white. One can almost smell the psychological twist involved when a James Baldwin or a LeRoi Jones[14] vilifies and baits white liberals who have championed the Negro's cause all their lives. So utterly

---

[13] Kwame Nkrumah (1909-1972), leader of Ghana and its predecessor state, Gold Coast, as well as the Lenin Peace Prize winner in 1963.
[14] Amiri Baraka (1934- ), formerly LeRoi Jones; American writer, professor, and critic.

convinced are Baldwin and Jones of the irremediable worth-lessness of the Negro people that anyone who thinks well of the Negro must seem to them simple-minded or simply dishonest.

To sum up: The Negro revolution is a fraud. It has no faith in the character and potentialities of the Negro masses. It has no taste for real enemies, real battlegrounds and desperate situations. It wants cheap victories and the easy way.

A genuine mass movement does not shy away from desperate situations. It wants above all to prove the validity and potency of its faith, and this it can do only by acting against overwhelming odds, so that whatever it achieves partakes of the miraculous. Indeed, where there are no difficulties the true revolutionary will deliberately create them, and it often looks as if the chief function of his faith is to get the revolutionary out of difficulties he himself created.

To conclude: The Negro with his imperishable alibi of "discrimination" has one freedom few of us have—the freedom to fail.

# The Aspirations of the New Poor

## February 25, 1968

Not all who are poor are frustrated. Some of the poor stagnating in the slums of the city are smug in their decay. They shudder at the thought of life outside their familiar cesspool. Even the respectable poor, when their poverty is of long standing, remain inert. They are awed by the immutability of the order of things. It takes a cataclysm—an invasion, a plague or some other communal disaster—to open their eyes to the transitoriness of the "eternal order."

It is usually those whose poverty is relatively recent, the "new poor," who throb with the ferment of frustration. The memory of better things is as fire in their veins. They are the disinherited and dispossessed who respond to every rising mass movement. It was the new poor in 17th century England who ensured the success of the Puritan Revolution. During the "movement of enclosure" thousands of landlords drove off their tenants and turned their fields into pastures. "Strong and active peasants, enamored of the soil that nurtured them, were transformed into wageworkers or sturdy beggars; ...city streets were filled with paupers." It was this mass of the dispossessed who furnished the recruits for Cromwell's[15] new-model army.

In Germany and Italy the new poor coming from a ruined middle class formed the chief support of the Nazi and Fascist revolutions. The potential revolutionaries in present-day England are not the workers but the disinherited civil servants and businessmen.

---

[15] Oliver Cromwell (1599-1658), English military and political leader.

**20**

This class has a vivid memory of affluence and dominion and is not likely to reconcile itself to straitened conditions and political impotence.

There have been of late, both here and in other countries, enormous periodic increases of a new type of new poor, and their appearance undoubtedly has contributed to the rise and spread of contemporary mass movements. Until recently the new poor came mainly from the propertied classes, whether in cities or on the land, but lately, and perhaps for the first time in history, the plain workingman appears in this role.

So long as those who did the world's work lived on a level of bare subsistence, they were looked upon and felt themselves as the traditionally poor. They felt poor in good times and bad. Depressions, however severe, were not seen as aberrations and enormities. But with the wide diffusion of a high standard of living, depressions and the unemployment they bring assumed a new aspect. The present-day workingman in the Western world feels unemployment as a degradation. He sees himself disinherited and injured by an unjust order of things and is willing to listen to those who call for a new deal.

★

The poor on the borderline of starvation have purposeful lives. To be engaged in a desperate struggle for food and shelter is to be wholly free from a sense of futility. The goals are concrete and immediate. Every meal is a fulfillment; to go to sleep on a full stomach is a triumph; and every windfall a miracle. What need could they have for "an inspiring super individual goal which would give meaning and dignity to their lives?" They are immune to the appeal of a mass movement.

Angelica Balabanoff[16] describes the effect of abject poverty on the revolutionary ardor of famous radicals who flocked to Moscow in the early days of the Bolshevik revolution. "Here I saw men and women who had lived all their lives for ideas, who had voluntarily renounced material advantages, liberty, happiness, and family affection for the realization of their ideals—completely absorbed by the problem of hunger and cold."

Where people toil from sunrise to sunset for a bare living, they nurse no grievances and dream no dreams. One of the reasons for the unrebelliousness of the masses in China is the inordinate effort required there to scrape together the means of the scantest subsistence. The intensified struggle for existence "is a static rather than a dynamic influence."

---

[16] Angelica Balabanoff (1878-1965), Jewish-Italian communist and activist.

# The Rude Awakening of Asia

## March 3, 1968

The crucial fact about the awakening in Asia, including Vietnam, is that it did not come from an accession of strength. It was not brought about by a gradual or sudden increase of material, intellectual, or moral powers, but by the shock of abandonment and exposure. It was an awakening brought about by a poignant sense of weakness. And we must know something about the mentality and potentialities of the present temper of the people of awakening Asia.

The rabid extremist in present-day Asia is usually a man of some education who has a horror of manual labor and who develops a mortal hatred for a social order that denies him a position of command. Every student, every minor clerk and officeholder, every petty member of the professions, feels himself one of the chosen.

It is these wordy, futile people who set the tone in Asia. Living barren, useless lives, they are without self-confidence and self-respect and their craving is for the illusion of weight and importance, and for the explosive substitutes of pride and faith.

It is chiefly to these pseudo-intellectuals that Communist Russia directs its appeal. It brings them the promise of membership in a ruling elite, the prospect of having a hand in the historical process and, by its doctrinaire double-talk, provides them with a sense of weight and depth.

As to the illiterate masses, the appeal of Communist preaching does not lie in its "truths," but in the vague impression it conveys to them that they and Russia are partners in some tremendous, unprecedented undertaking—the building of a proud future that will surpass and put to naught all "the things that are."

It has been often said that power corrupts. But it is perhaps equally important to realize that weakness, too, corrupts. Power corrupts the few, while weakness corrupts the many. Hatred, malice, rudeness, intolerance, and suspicion are the fruits of weakness.

The resentment of the weak does not spring from any injustice done to them but from the sense of their inadequacy and impotence. We cannot win the weak by sharing our wealth with them. They feel our generosity as oppression. St. Vincent de Paul cautioned his disciples to deport themselves so that the poor "will forgive you the bread you give them."

It is too late in the day for America to try to win anyone with words, and it is even more certain that we cannot win by giving. What then can we do? We can win the world only by example—by making our way of life as good as we know how. Our main problem is not the world but ourselves, and we can win the world only by overcoming ourselves.

# Man is the Squandered Resource

## March 10, 1968

I have always had the feeling that the people I live and work with are lumpy with talent. The cliché that talent is rare is not founded on fact. All that we know is that there are short periods in history when genius springs up all over the landscape, and long periods of mediocrity and inertness.

In the small city of Athens within the space of fifty years there sprang up a whole crop of geniuses—Aeschylus[17], Sophocles[18], Euripides[19], Phidias[20], Pericles[21], Socrates[22], Thucydides[23], Aristophanes.[24] These people did not come from heaven. Something similar happened in Florence at the time of the Renaissance,[25] in the Netherlands between 1400 and 1700 during the great period of Dutch-Flemish painting, and in Elizabethan England.[26]

What we know with certainty is not that talent and genius are rare exceptions but that all through history talent and genius have gone to waste on a vast scale.

Where the development of talent is concerned we are still at the food-gathering stage. We do not know how to grow it. Up to now in this country when one of the masses starts to write, paint,

---

[17] Aeschylus  (525-456 BC), ancient Greek tragedian.
[18] Sophocles (497-405 BC),  ancient Greek tragedian.
[19] Euripides (480-406 BC), ancient Greek tragedian.
[20] Phidias (480-430 BC), ancient Greek sculptor, painter, and architect.
[21] Pericles (495-429 BC), ancient Greek statesman and orator.
[22] Socrates (469-399 BC), ancient Greek philosopher.
[23] Thucydides (460-395 BC), ancient Greek historian.
[24] Aristophanes (446-386 BC), ancient Greek playwright of comedy.
[25] Renaissance, European cultural movement from the 14th to the 17th century.
[26] Elizabethan era (1558-1603), associated with the reign of Queen Elizabeth I.

etc., it is because he happens to bump into the right accident. In my case the right accident happened in the 1930s. I had the habit of reading from childhood, but very little schooling. I spent half of my adult life as a migratory worker and the other half as a long-shoreman.

The Hitler decade started me thinking, but there is an enormous distance between thinking and the act of writing. I had to acquire a taste for a good sentence—taste in the way a child tastes candy—before I stumbled into writing. Here is how it happened.

Late in 1936 I was on my way to do some placer mining near Nevada City, and I had a hunch that I would get snowbound. I had to get me something to read, something that would last me for a long time. So I stopped over in San Francisco to get a thick book. I did not really care what the book was about—history, theology, mathematics, farming, anything, as long as it was thick, and had small print and no pictures.

There was at that time a large secondhand bookstore on Market St. called Lieberman's and I went there to buy my book. I soon found one. It had about 1,000 pages of small print and no pictures. The price was $1. The title page said these were "The Essays of Michel de Montaigne." I knew what essays were but I did not know Montaigne from Adam. I put the book in my knapsack and caught the ferry to Sausalito.

Sure enough, I got snowbound. I read the book three times until I knew it almost by heart. When I got back to the San Joaquin Valley I could not open my mouth without quoting Montaigne, and the fellows liked it. It got so whenever there was an argument about anything—women, money, animals, food, death—they would ask: "What does Montaigne say?" I am quite sure that even now there must be a number of migratory workers up and down the San Joaquin Valley still quoting Montaigne.

★

I ought to add that the Montaigne edition I had was the John Florio translation. The spelling was modern, but the style seventeenth century—the style of the King James Bible and of Bacon's[27] Essays. The sentences have hooks in them which stick in the mind; they make platitudes sound as if they were new. Montaigne was not above anyone's head. Once in a workers' barrack near Stockton, the man in the next bunk picked up my Montaigne and read it for an hour or so. When he returned it he said: "Anyone can write a book like this."

The attempt to realize the potentialities of the masses may seem visionary and extravagant, yet it is eminently practical when judged by the criterion of social efficiency. For the efficiency of a society should be gauged not only by how effectively it utilizes its natural resources but by what it does with its human resources. Indeed, the utilization of natural resources can be deemed efficient only when it serves as a means for the realization of the intellectual, artistic, and manipulative capacities inherent in a population.

It is evident, therefore, that if we are to awaken and cultivate the talents dormant in a whole population we must change our conception of what is efficient, useful, practical, wasteful, and so on. Up to now in this country we are warned not to waste our time but we are brought up to waste our lives.

---

[27] Francis Bacon (1561-1626), English philosopher, statesman, and writer.

# The Western Mystery

March 17, 1968

The decline of the Occident has been proclaimed on housetops for over half a century. Knowledgeable people are still telling us that Europe is finished, America rotten to the core, and that the future is in Russia, China, India, Africa, and even in Latin America. We are urged to learn the meaning of life from these bearers of the future.

Yet it is becoming evident that if there is going to be anywhere a genuine growth of individual freedom and human dignity it will be from cuttings taken from the Occident. Even the Communist parties of the Occident are discovering that their historical role is not to change the Occident's way of life but to put a brake on the dehumanizing juggernaut of the Communist apparatus in Russia and China.

The fact is that the awakening of Asia and Africa has turned the Occident into a mystery. When we see to what ugly stratagems the new countries have to resort in order to make their people do the things which we consider natural and matter-of-fact we begin to realize how unprecedented the Occident is with its spontaneous enterprise and orderliness, and its elementary decencies. The mystery of our time is not the enigmatic Orient but the fantastic Occident.

The Occident is at present without fervent faith and hope. There is no overwhelming undertaking in sight that might set minds and hearts on fire. There is no singular happiness and no excessive suffering. We have already discounted every possible invention, and reduced momentous tasks to sheer routine. Though we are aware of deadly dangers ahead of us, our fears have not affected our rhythm of life. The Occident continues to function well at room temperature.

Now, there are those who maintain that lack of a strong faith must in the long run prove fatal to a society, and that the most decisive changes in history are those which involve a weakening or intensification of belief. Whether this be true or not it should be clear that a weakening of faith can be due as much to a gain in power, skill, and experience as to a loss of vigor and drive. Where there is the necessary skill and equipment to move mountains there is no need for the faith that moves mountains.

Intensification of belief is not necessarily a symptom of vigor, nor does a fading of belief spell decline. The strong, unless they are infected with a pathological fear, cannot generate and sustain a strong faith.

The Occident has skill, efficiency, orderliness, and a phenomenal readiness to work. It would be suicidal for the Occident to rely on a concocted new faith in a contest with totalitarian countries. We can prevail only by doing more and better what we know how to do well.

Free men are aware of the imperfection inherent in human affairs, and they are willing to fight and die for that which is not perfect. They know that basic human problems can have no final solutions, that our freedom, justice, equality, etc. are far from absolute, and that the good life is compounded of half measures, compromises, lesser evils, and gropings toward the perfect.

The rejection of approximations and insistence on absolutes are the manifestation of a nihilism that loathes tolerance and equality.

# A Kind Word for Intellectuals

## March 24, 1968

The incontestable fact is that the chronic carping of the militant intellectual has been a vital factor in the Occident's social progress. The blast of the intellectual's trumpets has not brought down or damaged our political and economic institutions. Napoleon predicted that ink would do to the modern social organization what cannon had done to the feudal system.

Actually, in the Occident, ink has acted more as a detergent than an explosive. It is doubtful whether without the activities of the pen-and-ink tribe the lot of the common people would be what it is now.

The events of the past 50 years have sharpened our awareness of the discrepancy between what the intellectual professes while he battles the status quo, and what he practices when he comes to power, and we are wont to search for the features of a commissar in the face of impassioned protest. Actually the metamorphosis of militant intellectual into commissar requires a specific cultural climate and, so far, has taken place mainly outside the Occident.

It is easy to underestimate the part played by Russia's and China's past in the evolvement of their present Marxist systems. A century ago Alexander Herzen[28] predicted that Russian communism would be Russian autocracy turned upside down. In China, where Mandarin intellectuals had the management of affairs in their keeping for centuries, the present dictatorship of an intellectocracy is more a culmination of, than a rupture with, the past.

---

[28] Alexander Herzen (1812-1870), Russian writer and thinker.

In Western Europe and the United States, where the tradition of individual freedom has deep roots in both the educated and the uneducated, the intellectuals cannot be self-righteous enough nor the masses submissive enough to duplicate the Russian and the Chinese experience. Thus in the Occident the militant intellectual is a stable type and a typical irritant; and whenever the influence of the Occident becomes strong enough the chronically disaffected intellectual appears on the scene and pits himself against the prevailing dispensation, even when it is a dispensation powered by his fellow intellectuals.

We see this illustrated in the present intellectual unrest in Eastern Europe and Russia, and it is beginning to seem that dominant Communist parties have more to fear from a Western infection than the Occident has to fear from Communist subversion.

Stalin's assertion that "no ruling class has managed without its own intelligentsia" applies of course to a totalitarian regime. A society that can afford freedom can also manage without a kept intelligentsia: It is vigorous enough to endure ceaseless harassment by the most articulate and perhaps most gifted segment of the population. Such harassment is the "eternal vigilance" which we are told is the price of liberty.

In a free society internal tensions are not the signs of brewing anarchy but the symptoms of vigor—the elements of a self-generating dynamism. Though there is no unequivocal evidence that the intellectual is at his creative best in a wholly free society, it is indubitable that his incorporation in, or close association with, a ruling elite sooner or later results in social and cultural stagnation.

The chronic frustration of the intellectual's hunger for power and lordship not only prompts him to side with the insulted and injured but may drive him to compensate for what he misses by realizing and developing his capacities and talents.

It goes without saying that to the typical intellectual the situation in the free world is a monstrous aberration. He cannot see how anyone can justify a state of affairs in which the gifted segment of the population is denied its heart's desire, while the masses go from strength to strength.

# A Century of Juveniles

**March 31, 1968**

To me one of the striking characteristics of the 20th century is its juvenility. Everywhere you look you see young and senile juveniles raising hell. No one can mistake the juvenile character of communism, fascism, racism, and the mass movements erupting at present in the backward parts of the world.

Nationalism has been called "the juvenile delinquency of the contemporary world." Almost all the leaders of the new or renovated countries have a pronounced juvenile element in their makeup. Every time you open a newspaper or a magazine you see the picture of a juvenile, black or white, shooting his mouth off.

And think of the senile delinquents like De Gaulle[29], Mao Tse-tung[30], Ho Chi Minh[31], Bertrand Russell[32], Benjamin Spock[33], and the retired candy-maker[34] who started the Birch movement.

Arthur Koestler[35] maintains that revolutionaries are perpetual juveniles, that there is something in them that keeps them from growing up. Now it is possible to see some family likeness between the adolescent who steps out of the warmth of the home into a cold world and knows not how to come to terms with things, and the revolutionary who refuses to come to terms with the status quo.

---

[29] Charles de Gaulle (1890-1970), French General and President.

[30] Mao Tse-tung (1863-1976), Chinese communist revolutionary and leader.

[31] Ho Chi Minh (1890-1969), Vietnamese Marxist revolutionary and leader.

[32] Bertrand Russell (1872-1970), British philosopher and social critic.

[33] Benjamin Spock (1903-1998), American pediatrician and author.

[34] Robert W. Welch (1899-1985), American businessman who in 1958 founded the John Birch Society, an American radical right-wing and advocacy group.

[35] Arthur Koestler (1905-1983), Hungarian author and essayist.

Then you look around you and you realize that the American go-getter, who certainly has no quarrel with the status quo, is as much a juvenile as any revolutionary. Finally, there is the juvenile character of most artists and writers. What quality can these diverse human types have in common?

The answer that suggests itself is that all the enumerated types have a vivid awareness of the possibility of a new beginning—of a sudden, drastic, miraculous change. To a mature person drastic change is not only something unpleasant, but he denies its reality. He sees drastic change, even when it seems a leap forward, as a falling on the face. When we get up we are back where we started, plus bruises and dishevelment.

The change that endures is that of growth—a change that proceeds quietly, and by degrees hardly to be perceived. To the juvenile mentality, continuity and gradualness are synonymous with stagnation, while drastic change is a mark of dynamism, vigor and freedom. To be fully alive is to feel that everything is possible.

The trouble is, of course, that juvenilization inevitably results in some degree of barbarization. We are up against the great paradox of the 20th century: namely, that a breakneck technological advance has gone hand in hand with a return to tribalism, charismatic leaders, medicine men, credulity, and tribal wars.

The juvenile, despite his professed idealism, is ruthless and extremist. His humanness is a precarious thing, easily sloughed off. Both the Bolshevists and the Fascists made use of juveniles to do the dirty work of killing.

The second half of the 20th century is seeing the dissolution of illusions, and the dimming of dreams and visions. Just as the 19th century saw the sapping of faith in God and in the kingdom of heaven, so the second half of the 20th century is seeing the weakening of faith in man, and in the possibility of a heaven on earth.

We are discovering that when dreams come true they may turn into nightmares.

# A Free Man Chooses to Work

## April 7, 1968

No one will claim that the majority of people in the Western world, be they workers or managers, find fulfillment in their work. But they do find in it a justification of their existence. The ability to do a day's work and get paid for it gives one a sense of usefulness and worth. The paycheck and the profitable balance sheet are certificates of value.

The significance of a job in the life of the Occidental individual is made particularly clear by the state of mind of the unemployed. There is little doubt that the frustration engendered by unemployment is due more to a corrosive sense of worthlessness, than to economic hardship. Unemployment pay, however adequate, cannot mitigate it.

In the Occident it is inaction rather than actual hardship which breeds discontent and disaffection. In America even legitimate retirement after a lifetime of work constitutes a fearsome crisis.

It is to be expected that where a sense of worth is attainable without effort, when one is born with it so to speak, the readiness to work is not likely to be pronounced. Thus in societies where the Negro race is officially designated as inferior, and every white person can feel himself a member of a superior race, the pressure of individual sell-assertion by work is considerably reduced. The presence of indolent "white trash" is usually a characteristic of such societies.

The remarkable thing is that the Occident's addiction to work is by no means synonymous with a love of work. The Western workingman actually has the illusion that he can kill work and be done with it.

The individualist society which manifests a marked readiness to work is one in which individualism is widely diffused.

Work, though it be hard and unceasing, is actually an easy solution of the problems which confront the autonomous individual, and it is not surprising that the individual in the mass should take this easy way out.

It is obvious, therefore that it is individual freedom which generates the readiness to work. On the face of it this is rather startling. It means that when the mass of people are free to work or not to work they usually act as if they are driven to work.

Freedom releases the energies of the masses not by exhilarating but by unbalancing, irritating and goading. You do not go to a free society to find carefree people.

When we leave people on their own, we are delivering them into the hands of a ruthless taskmaster from whose bondage there is no escape. The individual who has to justify his existence by his own efforts is in eternal bondage to himself.

# Escaping the Present

**April 14, 1968**

All around us today are young people forecasting doom, radicals forecasting revolution, and conservatives feeling the end of the world is upon them as a consequence. In such circumstances it is of interest to compare the attitudes toward present, future and past shown by the conservative, the liberal, the skeptic, the radical and the reactionary.

The conservative doubts that the present can be bettered, and he tries to shape the future in the image of the present. He goes to the past for reassurance about the present. He seeks a sense of continuity and the assurance that contemporary blunders are endemic in human nature. He wants to believe that new fads are very ancient heresies, that beloved things which are questioned have been equally threatened in the past.

The skeptic is like the conservative. To the skeptic the present is the sum of all that has been and shall be, and there is nothing new under the sun.

The liberal, on the other hand, sees the present as the legitimate offspring of the past and as constantly growing and developing toward an improved future: to damage the present is to maim the future. All three then cherish the present, and, as one would expect, they do not take willingly to the idea of its being radically altered.

The radical and the reactionary loathe the present. They see it as an aberration and a deformity. Both are ready to proceed ruthlessly and recklessly with the present, and both are hospitable to the idea of self-sacrifice. Wherein do they differ?

Primarily in their view of the malleability of man's nature. The radical has a passionate faith in the infinite perfectibility of human nature. He believes that by changing man's environment and by perfecting a technique of soul forming, a society can be wrought that is wholly new and unprecedented.

The reactionary does not believe that man has unfathomed potentialities for good in him. If a stable and healthy society is to be established, it must be patterned after the proven models of the past. He sees the future as a glorious restoration rather than an unprecedented innovation.

In reality the boundary line between radical and reactionary is not always distinct. The reactionary manifests radicalism when he comes to recreate his ideal past. His image of the past is based less on what it actually was than on what he wants the future to be. He innovates more than he reconstructs.

A somewhat similar shift occurs in the case of the radical when he goes about building his new world. He feels the need for practical guidance, and since he has rejected and destroyed the present he is compelled to link the new world with some point in the past. If he has to employ violence in shaping the new, his view of man's nature darkens and approaches closer to that of the reactionary.

What surprises one, when listening to the frustrated as they decry the present and all its works, is the enormous joy they derive from doing so. Such delight cannot come from the mere venting of a grievance. There must be something more—and there is.

By expatiating upon the incurable baseness and vileness of the times, the frustrated soften their feeling of failure and isolation. It is as if they said: "Not only our blemished selves, but the lives of all our contemporaries, even the most happy and successful, are worthless and wasted." Thus by deprecating the present they require a vague sense of equality.

# Presidential Material is Everywhere

## April 21, 1968

When I talk to American students and teachers about common Americans it is as if I was talking about mysterious people living on a mysterious continent.

They write books about us. They say we are a mass of brainless saps and automatic ghouls. Someone tells us how to vote, what to buy, how to live.

They ignore the fact that we elected Franklin D. Roosevelt[36] four times in the teeth of all the newspapers, in the teeth of Wall Street. And we elected Harry Truman[37] when all the newspapers said Thomas Dewey[38] was elected.

I remember the picture when Mr. Truman was sworn in—all the great brains standing around and wondering, "Look who is being sworn in as President."

Now the Trumans are a dime a dozen in this country. You can almost close your eyes, reach over to the sidewalk, and make a man President—and he'll turn out to be a Truman. Show me a society anywhere that can supply potential leaders like that. It's breathtaking.

---

[36] Franklin D. Roosevelt (1882-1945), 32nd U.S. President; served during the Great Depression and World War II.
[37] Harry S. Truman (1884-1972), 33rd U.S. President; succeeding Roosevelt after his death while in office in 1945.
[38] Thomas E. Dewey (1902-1971), former New York Governor; defeated in the U.S. Presidential election in both 1944 and 1948.

Who among the intellectuals would have predicted that a machine politician, patronized by the Knowlands[39] in Oakland, CA, would become Chief Justice Earl Warren[40]; that a hack politician endorsed by the Ku Klux Klan[41] would become Justice Hugo Black[42]; that a bankrupt haberdasher, who was given his start by the corrupt Pendergast[43] machine, would become President Harry Truman; that Lyndon Johnson[44], a Southern politician, would push through the civil rights legislation?

I have lived with Trumans and Johnsons all my life. To me they are the pride and the greatness of the country, and they know how to defend it. When a Johnson gets a job you do not presume to tell him how to do it. You have faith in his competence, and his capacity to learn. You know he will do whatever he does the best way he knows how. You also know that the Johnsons don't scare, and will not swerve from their path.

It is the unique greatness of this country that it has many Trumans and Johnsons. To us, a Johnson in the White House is not a hero, but one of us, saddled with the toughest job in the world, and trying to do his best. If he fails, we fail; if he succeeds, we succeed.

---

[39] Knowland was a political family centered in Oakland, CA, founded by Joseph R. Knowland (1873-1966).
[40] Earl Warren (1891-1974), U.S. Supreme Court Justice, 1952 to 1969.
[41] Ku Klux Klan or "KKK" is a white supremacist organization established during the 1860s in the wake of the American Civil War.
[42] Hugo LaFayette Black (1886-1971), U.S. Supreme Court Justice, 1937 to 1971.
[43] Thomas J. Pendergast (1873-1945), former political boss of Kansas City, MI.
[44] Lyndon B. Johnson (1908-1973), 36th U.S. President; succeeding Kennedy after his assassination in 1961.

# The Nature of Creativity

April 28, 1968

The creative impulse does not flash forth when necessity takes us by the throat. The desperate struggle for existence is a static rather than a dynamic influence. The urgent search for the vitally necessary is likely to stop once we have found something that is more or less adequate, but the search for the superfluous has no end.

Men never philosophize or tinker more freely than when they know that their speculation or tinkering leads to no weighty results. We are more ready to try the untried when what we do is inconsequential. Hence the remarkable fact that many inventions had their birth as toys.

When we find that a critical challenge has apparently evoked a marked creative response, there is always the possibility that the response came not from people cornered by a challenge but from people who, in an exuberance of energy, went out in search of a challenge.

It is worth remembering that the discovery of America was a byproduct of the search for ginger, cloves, pepper, and cinnamon. The utilitarian device, even when it is an essential ingredient of our daily life, is most likely to have its ancestry in the nonutilitarian.

On the whole it seems to be true that the creative periods in history were buoyant and even frivolous. One thinks of the light-heartedness of Periclean Athens[45], the Renaissance, the Elizabethan Age, and the Age of the Enlightenment.[46]

Man shares his playfulness with other warm-blooded animals, with mammals and birds. Cold-blooded animals (insects, reptiles, etc.) do not play. Equally significant is the duration of the propensity to play. Mammals and birds play only when young, while man retains the propensity to play throughout life. My feeling is that the tendency to carry youthful characteristics into adult life is at the root of man's uniqueness in the universe.

Man is the only young thing in the world. A deadly seriousness emanates from all other forms of life. The cry of pain and of fear man has in common with other forms of life, but he alone can smile and laugh.

To remember how fruitful the playful mood can be is to be immune to the propaganda of the untalented which puts a high value on resentment as a fuel of achievement.

The untalented writer or artist who cannot achieve uniqueness by realizing his capacities must act out a unique life. These form a world or their own, a brotherhood of resentment. To be alienated becomes a mark of intellectual and artistic distinction, and to revile the society they live in an initiation into the mysteries of the universe.

---

[45] Periclean Athens refers to the Greek city-state from 480BC-404BC.

[46] Enlightenment era or "Age of Reason," post-Renaissance western cultural expansion in the 18th century, in which reason was advocated over authority.

# Rioting is Fruitless, Corrupts Society

## May 5, 1968

We are being brainwashed about the riots. We are told that the riots are good for the Negro's soul; that they give him a feeling of manhood. We are also told that the riots are a deserved punishment for the white man's sin of racism.

The police are commended for their restraint. The black-power loudmouths, close kin of Doc Duvalier's[47] murder boys, the Ton Ton Macoutes in Haiti, are free to do as they please. We are supposed to be thankful that the burning and looting last only a few days.

Who are the rioters? They are Negro juveniles of all ages for whom the riots are a ball, and Negro criminals for whom the riots are a windfall. The decent, hardworking Negroes in the middle are intimidated by the reckless juveniles and criminals, and remain voiceless. But they vote.

My feeling is that a candidate who, when addressing a Negro audience, states unequivocally that he will prevent rioting by every means, even if he has to shoot every looter, will get the Negro vote.

If the riots are allowed to become a part of our pattern of life, the consequences are likely to be disastrous. Sooner or later we shall discover the fact that has been staring us in the face; namely, that there is hardly any rioting in the South.

Once this fact sinks in, a profitable new industry will be born in the South; the readying and packaging of police forces,

---

[47] François "Papa Doc" Duvalier (1907-1971), President of Haiti from 1957-1971; his nickname refers to success with fighting diseases of the day.

complete with Bull Connors[48], cattle prods, and bloodhounds, for exportation to the North.

The Negro riots are a plowing and harrowing of the Northern cities for the transplantation of the South to the North. The South is being transplanted not by white racists but by Negroes.

The genuinely humane people who say that riots are unavoidable, that they will cease when every Negro wrong has been righted, and every white heart is cleansed of prejudice and selfishness, are not aiding the Negro but are hastening the corruption and debasement of our society.

---

[48] Term referring to Theophilus Eugene "Bull" Connor's use of fire hoses to fight race riots in Alabama; practice is historically noted as a symbol of bigotry.

# The Rise of the Intellectual

**May 12, 1968**

The present Americanization of the world is an unprecedented phenomenon. The penetration of a foreign influence has almost always depended on the hospitableness of the educated and the well-to-do. Yet worldwide diffusion of American habits, fashion, and ways proceeds in the teeth of shrill opposition of intellectuals everywhere and the hostility of the better people.

The only analogy which comes to mind is the early spread of Christianity, with the difference that Americanization is not being pushed by apostles and missionaries but like a chemical reagent penetrates of its own accord, and instantly combines with the common people and the young. "The American way of life," says a British observer, "has become the religion of the masses in five continents."

Ironically, at a time when the world is being Americanized the American intellectual seems to be seceding from America. Here in the San Francisco Bay area, the dramatic change in the intellectual's attitude toward America has the earmarks of a historical turning point.

The first impression is that the American intellectual is being Europeanized, and one is tempted to see a connection between influencing and being influenced: that by influencing the world America unavoidably opens itself up to foreign influences; and in this case, as so often before, the intellectual is the carrier of the foreign influence.

Actually, the intellectual's revulsion from contemporary America has little to do with the penetration of a foreign influence but is the result of a recent change in the tilt of the social landscape. The nature of a society is largely determined by the direction in which talent and ambition flow—by the tilt of the social landscape.

.

In America, until recently, most of the energy, ability, and ambition found its outlet in business. In *Notes of a Son and Brother* Henry James[49] tells how, as children, he and his brother William were mortified that their father was not a businessman but a philosopher and author. In a European country like France, where writers and artists rank high in public esteem, boys and girls probably find it humiliating to admit that their father is a mere businessman and not a writer or an artist.

Now, the important fact is that since Sputnik the prestige and material rewards of intellectual pursuits have risen sharply in this country, and the social landscape has begun to tilt away from business. Right now the career of a scientist or a professor can be more exciting than that of a businessman, and its material rewards are not be to sneered at.

A recent survey showed that only 20% of undergraduates intend to go into business. The chances are great therefore that at present many individuals with superb talents for wheeling and dealing are pawing their way up the academic ladder or are throwing their weight around in literary and artistic circles. This is a state of affairs not unlike that which prevails in France, hence the impression that the American intellectual is being Europeanized.

★

There is no telling how soon and to what degree the diversion of talent and ambition from business might make itself felt in a diminution of economic venturesomeness and drive. Nor can we tell whether the inflow of energies into intellectual pursuits will

---

[49] Henry James (1843-1916), American novelist.

result in an upsurge of cultural creativeness. But it is beyond doubt that the movers and shakers are already at work inside and outside the universities.

The civil rights movement and the Vietnam War are ideal vehicles for these would-be makers of history. Making history is a substitute for making a million dollars. The book of history seems to lie open and every two-bit intellectual wants to turn its pages.

# Man's Destiny is in the City

### May 19, 1968

For 18 years, as a migratory farm worker and placer miner, I knew nature at close quarters. Nature was breathing down my neck, and I knew it did not like me. If I stretched on the ground to rest, nature pushed its hard knuckles into my side, and sent bugs, burrs, and foxtails to make me get up and be gone. As a placer miner I had to run the gantlet of buckbrush, manzanita, and poison oak when I left the road to find my way to a creek.

Direct contact with nature almost always meant scratches, bites, torn clothes, and grime that ate its way into every pore of the body. On the paved road, even when miles from anywhere, I felt at home. I had a sense of kinship with the winding, endless road that cares not where it goes and what its load. And the road led to the city.

I knew with every fiber of my being that the city only was man's home on this planet; that it was his refuge from a hostile non-human cosmos. I did not have to be a scholar to recognize that man's greatest achievements were conceived and realized, not in the bracing atmosphere of the plains, deserts, forests and mountaintops, but in the smelly, noisy, overcrowded cities of Jerusalem, Athens, Florence, Shakespeare's[50] London and Rembrandt's[51] Amsterdam.

There is in this country, particularly among the educated, a romantic, worshipful attitude toward nature. Nature is thought to

---

[50] William Shakespeare (1564-1616), English poet and playwright.
[51] Rembrandt van Rijn (1606-1669), Dutch painter and artist.

be pure, innocent, serene, health-giving, the fountainhead of elevated thoughts and feelings.

When some years ago I wrote an article in which I questioned nature's benevolence and suggested that the contest between man and nature has been the central drama of the universe, I was rewarded with a shower of brickbats.

My hunch is that the attitude of the educated American toward nature is shaped and colored by European literature. Europe is probably one of the tamest parts of the world. Imagine a subcontinent without a single desert or rampaging river, without tornadoes, sandstorms, hailstorms or inundations.

Compare it with our snarling continent. Open your newspaper any morning and you find reports of floods, tornadoes, blizzards, hurricanes, hailstorms, avalanches, eruptions, pests and plagues.

Fly over this continent and you see what we have done. We have cast a net of concrete roads over a snarling continent, and proceeded to tame each square. Every once in a while there is a heaving and rumbling, and the savage continent shakes us off its back.

The miracle is that we have taken a continent unfit for human beings and made it a cornucopia of unprecedented plenty. The wilderness boys accuse us of ravaging and raping a virgin continent. Actually, our enormous mastery over nature is such that if we were so minded we could, in 50 years or so, regrow all the forests, replenish the soil, cleanse all rivers and the air of pollution, have buffalo herds again thundering on the plains, and make the continent as virgin as when we first got here.

If this nation decays and declines it will be not because we have raped and ravaged a continent, but because we do not know how to build and run viable cities. America's destiny will be decided in the city.

# Israel's Lonely Position

**May 26, 1968**

The Jews are a peculiar people: Things permitted to other nations are forbidden to the Jews.

Other nations drive out thousands, even millions of people and there is no refugee problem. Russia did it; Poland and Czechoslovakia did it; Turkey drove out a million Greeks, and Algeria a million Frenchmen; Indonesia threw out heaven knows how many Chinese—and no one says a word about refugees.

But in the case of Israel, the displaced Arabs have become eternal refugees. Everyone insists that Israel must take back every single Arab. Arnold Toynbee[52] calls the displacement of the Arabs an atrocity greater than any committed by the Nazis.

Other nations when victorious on the battlefield dictate peace terms. But when Israel is victorious it must sue for peace. Everyone expects the Jews to be the only real Christians in this world.

Other nations when they are defeated survive and recover. But should Israel be defeated it would be destroyed. Had Nasser[53] triumphed last June he would have wiped Israel off the map, and no one would have lifted a finger to save the Jews.

No commitment to the Jews by any government, including our own, is worth the paper it is written on. There is a cry of outrage all over the world when people die in Vietnam or when two Negroes are executed in Rhodesia. But when Hitler slaughtered Jews no one remonstrated with him.

---

[52] Arnold Toynbee (1889-1975), English economic historian and social activist.
[53] Fu'ad Nassar (1914-1976), Palestinian communist party leader and activist.

The Swedes, who are ready to break off diplomatic relations with America because of what we do in Vietnam, did not let out a peep when Hitler was slaughtering Jews. They sent Hitler choice iron ore, and ball bearings, and serviced his troop trains to Norway.

The Jews are alone in the world. If Israel survives, it will be solely because of Jewish efforts. And Jewish resources.

Yet at this moment Israel is our only reliable and unconditional ally. We can rely more on Israel than Israel can rely on us. And one has only to imagine what would have happened last summer had the Arabs and their Russian backers won the war to realize how vital the survival of Israel is to America and the West in general.

I have a premonition that will not leave me; as it goes with Israel so will it go with all of us. Should Israel perish the holocaust will be upon us.

Israel must live!

# Colleges Aren't for Kids

### June 9, 1968

Someone asked me why there are so many dogs on the Berkeley campus. My answer was that where there are kids there are dogs. This flippant answer actually contains a serious formulation of the chief trouble that is plaguing every campus in the land.

Universities are made for men, not for kids. Kids do not want to learn; they want to teach, and they want to act. To kids, the need to learn is proof of their inadequacy and inferiority. A university is the least fit place for kids to prove their manhood.

What then is the solution? The obvious answer is that kids should not be allowed on the campus. You must arrange things so that kids can prove their manhood before they go to college. We have no puberty rites in this country. The only way kids can prove their manhood is by doing a man's work and earning a man's wages.

On leaving high school at the age of 17 every boy and girl should be given an opportunity, or even be compelled, to spend three years earning a living at top wages. Government and business must cooperate in seeing to it that every high school graduate has a good job waiting for him.

There is an enormous backlog of work to be done inside and outside our cities. Arrangements will have to be made for the mass importing of skills. We must dovetail our difficulties into opportunities for growth.

If after three years of work the high school graduate wants to go to college, the entrance requirements would be an ability to read and write, and proof that he has earned, a living for three years and saved enough money to carry through.

With a student body made up of grown men and women universities could become what they are supposed to be: places to learn at leisure, unhurried by examination and supervision, free to swim or sink.

The word school comes from the Greek schole which means leisure. The examinations at the end of four years will tell what the student has learned and what he is qualified for; and the diploma will state these facts.

To have kids on the campus is to create an exclusive situation of delayed manhood. When children are not allowed to grow to manhood they do not remain children but become childish. A child one year old is older than the oldest adolescent on the campus.

# Student Challenge: Grow Up

**June 16, 1968**

Never has youth been face to face with more breathtaking opportunities and more deadly influences. Never before has character been so decisive a factor in the survival of the young. Nowadays, a 12-year-old child must be possessed of a strong character in order not to get irrevocably blemished and flawed.

The road from boyhood to manhood has become sieve-like: Those without the right size of character slip into pitfalls and traps. The rate of failure in the present young generation will be astronomical. The supposedly most sheltered generation is actually the most exposed.

The society of the young is at present almost as subject to the laws of sheer survival as any animal society. In the San Francisco Bay area you can see the young beset and preyed upon by vultures, wolves and parasites: dope peddlers, pimps, lechers, perverts, thugs, cult mongers, and ideological seducers. Everywhere you look you can see human beings rot before they ripen.

The young refuse to grow up but they do not stay young. Our campuses are becoming dour, playless nurseries, echoing with doctrinaire baby talk. You see six-foot babies clamoring for dominion and power, and protesting against universities not having adequate arrangements for child care.

The young are not going anywhere, yet they are impatient. They cannot bide their time because it is not the time of their growth. We are discovering that power corrupts idealistic adolescents more than it does materialistic adults. Twenty-five centuries ago the prophet Isaiah described the Lord's punishment of a corrupt society: "And I will make boys their princes, and babes shall rule over them... the youth will be insolent to his elder and the base fellow to the honorable."

It is well to remember that the student revolutionaries are not only overgrown babies but also self-styled two-bit intellectuals. The student revolt is a phase in the revolt of the intellectuals against a middle-class dominated industrial society—a revolt that has been going on for over a century.

In the countries between the Elba and the China Sea you can see the global slum that comes into being when militant intellectuals have the power to make their visions and dreams come true. You wonder what an America dominated by the Students for a Democratic Society (SDS)[54] would be like.

They tell us that middle-class America is a pig heaven, and they want no part of it. But judging by what they are doing at San Francisco State College and at Columbia University you know that if the Students for A Democratic Society have their way they would turn America into a pigsty.

---

[54] Students for a Democratic Society (SDS) was a activist movement in 1960s, generally regarded as the longest-standing and most effective of its type.

# Man Works Hard for Toys

**June 23, 1968**

All my working life I have been interested in the question of the readiness to work. In this country, of course, the problem is not how to induce people to work but how to find enough jobs for people who want to work. But in the Communist world, the chief preoccupation of every government between the Elbe and the China Sea is how to make people work—how to induce them to plow, sow, harvest, build, manufacture, work in mines, and so forth. It confronts them day in and day out, and it shapes not only their domestic policies but their relations with the outside world.

Thus the goings on inside the Communist world serve to remind us that our readiness to work, so far from being natural and normal, is strange and unprecedented. That free men should be willing to work day after day, even after their vital needs are satisfied, and that work should be seen as a mark of uprighteousness and manly worth, is something that remains more or less incomprehensible to many people outside this country and Western Europe.

Sociologists and psychologists have given many profound and erudite reasons for the Occident's fabulous readiness to work. These reasons are no doubt valid, but they are not the main ones. To me the most significant fact is that there is a greater readiness to work in a society with a high standard of living than with a low one. The point is that we are more ready to strive for superfluities than for necessities.

To put it bluntly: The readiness to work springs from trivial and questionable motives. I can remember Paul-Henri Spaak[55] saying after World War II that in order to energize the Belgian workers for the stupendous task of reconstruction and recovery he had to fill the shops and tease the people with all the "luxuries and vices" they had been accustomed to.

Atlee[56], a better socialist but a lesser statesman, instituted at that time in Britain a policy of "Socialist austerity," and the reluctance of British workers to exert themselves beyond a certain limit has handicapped Britain's postwar economy. There is a traditional low standard of living among the British workers. The lack of an intense desire for things among the masses (one might say the reasonableness of the masses) is holding production down.

A vigorous society is apparently a society made up of people who set their hearts on toys. The self-righteous moralists decry such a society, yet it is well to keep in mind that to both children and artists luxuries are more necessary than necessities. He who does not know that in human affairs the trivial is not the trivial has missed a chief clue to man's nature.

It is not true that a society need a lofty purpose and a shining vision to achieve much. Both in the marketplace and on the battlefield men who set their hearts on toys have often displayed unequalled initiative and drive. And one must be ignorant of the creative process to look for a close correspondence between motive and achievement in the world of thought and imagination.

At a time when Britain's economic difficulties have assumed catastrophic proportions, its novelists, poets, playwrights, compos-

---

[55] Paul-Henri Spaak (1899-1872), Beligain socialist and politician.
[56] Clement Richard Altee (1883-1967), British Prime Minister from 1945-1951.

ers, artists, scientists and technologists are performing as brilliantly as ever before.

Most history books tell us that the vigor of a society depends upon the temper and performance of its superior individuals. It is the elite in all fields that generate the impulses which energize the mass of people and keep a society rigorous and striving. But the events in Britain at this moment are demonstrating that the health and drive of a society depend upon the temper, habits and attitudes of the common people.

# A Blur in De Gaulle's Grand Vision

## June 30, 1968

What lessons can we learn from the latest upheaval in France?

It is now obvious that De Gaulle's vision of an Imperial France playing the part of a great power in the atomic age cannot evoke enthusiasm in a majority of Frenchmen.

The ebbing of nationalism in the Western world is one of the most fateful consequences of the second World War. Indeed, right now nationalism has become a specialty of the backward countries, and of minorities that feel held back or persecuted.

The fact that De Gaulle is a great man gives to the events in France an unprecedented demonstrative quality. They demonstrate that in Europe at this moment history is made by circumstances and not by great men.

Right now it is the unification of Europe that can make men truly great; can cure the social and economic ills which beset any European nation; and can ward off any danger that threatens Europe from without.

The events in France have also taught us that when the middle musters its hundreds of thousands, as the supporters of De Gaulle did on the Champs Elysees, the spectacle dampens the fervor of the extremists.

When the majority becomes visible and audible, the extremist minorities see what they are up against and have second thoughts.

Finally we have learned that the idealistic form of juvenile delinquency is a most explosive threat to social stability, and that universities are the place where the detonation is most readily set off. It is now clear that students under 20 crave spectacular action, and unless this craving finds an outlet in useful activities it will vent itself in revolutionary turmoil.

The young must be given, as early as possible, a chance to show what they can do on their own. They want scope to live "a life of ideas," but even more an opportunity to plan, build and experiment—to act first and learn as they go.

Might it not be possible to have a territory within each country where the young would have all power and responsibility, and where no one over 30 would be allowed to stay?

# Creativity in the Masses

July 9, 1968

The great struggles of the 20th century have been struggles between freedom and oppression, yet it is not always clear who benefits from being free. The interesting thing is that the energizing effect of freedom seems confined to the masses. Freedom releases the energies of the masses not by exhilarating but by unbalancing, irritating, and goading.

You do not go to a free society to find carefree people. When you leave common people on their own, you are delivering them into the hands of an inner taskmaster from whose bondage there is no escape. The energies thus liberated are usually directed toward the accomplishment of practical works, and not towards cultural or artistic achievements.

It is not at all certain that individual freedom is a vital factor in the release of creative energies in literature, art, music, and science. Many of the outstanding achievements in these fields were not realized in an atmosphere of absolute freedom. Certainly, in this country cultural creativeness has not been proportionate to our degree of individual freedom.

★

There is a chronic insecurity at the core of the creative person, and he needs a milieu that will nourish his confidence and sense of uniqueness. Discerning appreciation and a modicum of deference and acclaim are probably more vital for his creative flow than freedom to fend for himself. Thus a despotism that recognizes and subsidizes excellence might be more favorable for the performance of the artist than a free society that does not take him seriously.

Coleridge[57] protested that "the darkest despotisms on the continent have done more for the growth and elevation of the fine arts than the English government. A great musical composer in Germany and Italy is a great man in society and a real dignity and rank are conceded him. So it is with the sculptor or painter or architect. In this country there is no general reverence for the fine arts."

It is of course conceivable that a wholly free society might become imbued with a reverence for the fine arts, but up to now the indications have been that where common folk have room enough there is not much room for the dignity and rank of the typical writer or artist.

The vital question is whether the masses can create anything worthwhile on their own. What would happen if common folk, living their common lives, were to be infused with appreciation of the beautiful and allowed to acquire a certain expertise in all the arts?

We know of one instance in the past where the masses entered the field of cultural creativeness not as mere onlookers but as participants. We are told that Florence at the time of the Renaissance had more artists than citizens. Where did these artists come from? They were mostly the sons of artisans, shopkeepers, peasants, and petty officials. The art honored in Florence was a trade, and the artists were treated as artisans. Craftsmen and their workshops played a vital role in the unfolding of the new painting and sculpture.

---

[57] Samuel Taylor Coleridge (1772-1834), English poet, critic, and philosopher.

The Renaissance was born in the marketplace. Almost all the great artists were apprenticed when children to craftsmen. Everyday life was permeated by an interest in the procedure and technique of the arts. At the same time, even the greatest of the Florentine painters and sculptors had an intimate contact with the world's work, and lacked the disdain of the practical characteristic of the artists of ancient Greece and of our time.

Obviously, a participation of the masses in cultural creativeness seems more feasible when we think of turning them into creative craftsmen rather than into artists and literati.

# Intellectual Rejection of America

## July 14, 1968

San Francisco is a city of conventions, and many of the participants visit the waterfront.

It is of absorbing interest to watch doctors, bankers, manufacturers, technicians, get into talk with longshoremen particularly during the lunch hour.

As you listen to the easy conversation you realize how many topics there are in which people from all walks of life in this country are equally interested, and on which they can all talk with some expertise. I can't think of any other country where you will find such easy intercourse between different segments of the population.

Imagine, then, my surprise when I read recently what Mary McCarthy[58] told an interviewer of the British Broadcasting Corp. She had just returned from Vietnam. While waiting for a plane at an airfield, this distinguished American writer could not strike up a conversation with any of the American soldiers around her. This, she told the reporter, is the most uneducated army America has ever had.

Obviously, something has been happening to the American intellectual in recent years. He is becoming more and more like intellectuals elsewhere; which is to say, he is becoming more exclusive and aristocratic.

---

[58] Mary McCarthy (1912-1989), American author, critic, and political activist, who favored the Vietcong during the Vietnam War.

Now, in other countries the intellectual's disdain of common folk need not have weighty consequences. A Burke[59] who spoke of the swinish masses could yet glory in England's greatness. But in an America imbued with the spirit and tastes of the masses, revulsion from common people goes hand in hand with a rejection of the country.

Nowhere else in the world present do intellectuals reject and defame their society as do intellectuals in America. "A pig heaven," "a monster with 200 million heads," "an air-conditioned nightmare," and "a cancer on the body of mankind" are some of the epithets.

Anyone who speaks well of America is accused of "intellectual treason." The savage attack masquerades as a battle for peace. Actually it is a battle for America's unconditional defeat.

And the total estrangement from their society has endowed these self-appointed saviors of humanity with a peculiar viciousness. They are experts at character assassination, and they displayed their expertise to the full in the venomous attacks on President Johnson.

Al Capp[60] said recently that although he has been for years a critic of American society it has only been since he began poking fun at pacifists that he has felt any fear for his life.

---

[59] Edmund Burke (1729-1797), Anglo-Irish statesman and philosopher who wrote of the "swinish multitude" and the threat of "mass literacy."

[60] Al Capp (1909-1979), American cartoonist and humorist; best know for the *Li'l Abner* comic strip.

# Imitators Reject Their Model

**July 21, 1968**

The rapid modernization of a backward country is basically a process of imitation—the backward country imitates an advanced model. And it is an indication of the fantastic quality of man's nature that such an apparently harmless process should often become convulsive and explosive.

Contrary to what one would expect, it is easier for the advanced to imitate the backward than the other way around. The backward see in imitation an act of submission and a proof of their inadequacy. They must rid themselves of their sense of inferiority, must demonstrate their prowess, before they will open their minds and hearts to all that the world can teach them.

Most often in history it was the conqueror who learned willingly from the conquered. There is, therefore, a kernel of practicalness in the preposterous attempt of a Nasser or a Sukarno[61] to turn their people into warriors. It is a fact that nations with a warrior tradition such as the Japanese, or the inheritors of Genghis Khan[62] in Outer Mongolia, find modernization less difficult than nations of subjected peasants such as Russia and China. It is also plausible that the defeat of 40 million Arabs by tiny Israel is rendering modernization of the Arab world more difficult and painful.

---

[61] Sukarno (1901-1970), President of Indonesia from 1945 to 1967.
[62] Genghis Khan (1162-1227), founder of the Mongol Empire.

It is of course to be expected that imitation will be relatively free of resentment when it is possible for the imitators to identify themselves wholeheartedly with their model. It is the great misfortune of our time that in the present surge of Westernization so many factors combine to keep the awakening countries from identifying themselves with the West they imitate.

The fresh memory of colonialism, the color line, the difference in historical experience, the enormous gap in living standards, the fear of the educated minority in the backward countries that democracy and free enterprise would rob them of their birthright to direct, plan, and supervise—all these combine to create an attitude of suspicion and antagonism toward the West.

One could also expect that imitation would be least impeded when we are made to feel that our act of imitation is actually an act of becoming the opposite of that which we imitate. Communism can be an effective agency for the transmission of Western achievements to backward countries because it convinces the backward that by modernizing themselves they are actually becoming the opposite of the capitalist model they imitate.

Finally, it is obvious that the imitators would be most at ease when they imitate a defeated or dead model. Hence the impulse of the imitators to defeat or even destroy the model they imitate.

★

An awareness that rapid modernization is essentially a process of imitation should help us not only to make sense of the turmoil in the backward countries, but also to gauge the durability of all that is being achieved there at present.

When we see how wholly different the social and political conditions are in the underdeveloped countries from what they had been in Europe and America at the birth of the machine age, it is natural to wonder whether the transplantation of Western achievement to these countries is likely to be viable. However, when we keep in mind that what we are observing is an act of concerted imitation, the view changes completely. Conditions optimal for origination are not necessarily optimal for imitation.

Origination requires a more or less loose social order. In which the individual has leeway to tinker, follow his hunches, and run risks on his own. On the other hand, rapid imitation is facilitated by social compactness, regimentation, and concerted action. Thus the collectivist bias of the backward countries may be an aid rather than a hindrance in their race to catch up with the West.

# The Silent Majority

July 28, 1968

Everywhere we look in the world at present we see something trying to be born. It is so in Latin America and in Canada, in Asia and in Africa. The demonstrations and riots in this country are the accompaniments of a new birth.

A pregnant, swollen world is writhing in labor, and everywhere untrained quacks are officiating as obstetricians. These quacks say that the only way the new can be born is by a Cesarean operation; they lust to rip the belly of the world open.

There is a cult of violence in the land. Whereas in former times violence in everyday affairs had been a characteristic of the uncivilized and the brutalized, we now find scholars, writers, poets, artists and students glorying in the apocalyptic spectacle of burned and looted cities, in the anarchic turmoil on the campuses, and in the general disruption of law and order.

The executive director[63] of the American Civil Liberties Union in New York chides policemen for their ungentlemanly treatment of violent demonstrators. New York policemen, he says, "often become as violent as the demonstrators."

According to this self-appointed savior of humanity the function of the police is to protect the demonstrators, and make society safe for violence. In Newark where rowdy student demonstrators from Rutgers had to put up with hecklers, the Civil Liberties Union accused the police of "inaction."

---

[63] William Kunstler (1919-1995), American attorney and civil rights activist; ACLU director from 1964 to 1972.

70

Ours is an age of minorities. The two-bit idealists who foam at the mouth about freedom and democracy are actually minocrats. They tell us that a society is free only when its minorities are free to box the ears of the majority.

Rule by majority, they say, is tyranny. They echo Khrushchev[64] who opposed free elections in Eastern Germany because it would mean that "the majority, not truth, triumphed."

You wonder when and how the majority will stand up against the minorities that besmirch and torment it. Does the decent, hardworking majority ever lose patience? Does it strike back of its own accord?

My feeling is that if the majority does not deal forcefully with those who mistake our forbearance with weakness we shall be trampled underfoot by an unholy alliance between the extremists of the left and of the right.

We in the middle must kick in the teeth of the rowdy leftist nincompoops, and of the black power[65] murder boys, if we are to prevent the coming to power of the Joe McCarthys[66] or even the Hitlers. We need mayors of cities and presidents of universities who will delight in the battle, and will make it impossible for cowardly rowdies to win easy victories over tame enemies on tame battlegrounds.

---

[64] Nikita Khrushchev (1894-1971), Soviet Union leader from 1953 to 1964.
[65] "Black Power" was a racialist slogan and movement, emerging in the 1960s.
[66] Joseph Raymond McCarthy (1908-1957), American politician; most famous for heightening public fears of Communist subversion during the Cold War.

# Educated Want to be Taken Seriously

## August 4, 1968

I sometimes wonder what government and life in general would be like if voting were restricted to the formally educated—to those with a college degree. Gandhi[67] once said that what worried him most was the hardness of heart of the educated. It staggers the mind that education rather than educating the heart often makes it more savage.

Think of the scurrilous savagery directed against the character of L.B.J.[68] by some of the best educated people in this country. Nor can I forget that it was the best educated nation in the world that produced Hitler and Nazism, and invented the gas chambers. In Stalin's Russia professors, writers, artists, and scientists kowtowed and abased themselves daily before one of the most brutal tyrants the world has seen. The Stalin cult was the work of the educated.

And what sort of nation would we have on this continent if only college graduates had been allowed to enter America? One thing is certain: There would have been not one U.S.A. but a mosaic of lingual and cultural groups biting and fighting each other. It was due to the fact that the majority of the immigrants were the lowest and the poorest, the despised and the rejected, that

---

[67] Mohandas Gandhi (1869-1948), Indian political leader during independence movment from Britian.
[68] Lyndon Baines Johnson (1908-1973), 36th President of the United States.

the heterogeneous millions blended rapidly and thoroughly into one mighty nation.

It is probably true that the political health of this country has been due partly to our withholding of power from the intellectuals, and to not heeding their political views. Where, as in France, intellectuals play a leading role in political life, parliamentary government becomes chaotic. The vindictive bickering of the many cliques and splinter-groups creates a bedlam atmosphere inimical to political stability. The denouement is dictatorship—the alternative to anarchy.

So far parliamentary government by intellectuals has worked only in small countries, where the divisiveness and internecine strife characteristic of intellectuals in power are kept within limits by the tangible, pressing problem of national survival. The instances that come to mind are Sweden, Finland and Israel. In Israel, parliamentary government has endured mainly as a result of a state of siege. If the pressure of the Arab world were to cease, political life in Israel might be reduced to near anarchy.

The Anglo-Saxon type of democracy has shown itself to be an effective instrument for the government of large countries. One of the chief problems which now confront the large democracies is how to contain their militant, Latin-Americanized intellectuals.

The intellectual wants to be listened to. He wants to instruct and be taken seriously. It is more important to him to be important than to be free. He would rather be persecuted than ignored. The freedom he has here to say whatever he pleases seems to him a jester's freedom. He actually envies intellectuals in Communist countries who are persecuted by governments that take intellectuals seriously.

# Czechoslovakia & Socialist Lethargy

## August 11, 1968

In the period between the two world wars Czechoslovakia was one of the most progressive and prosperous nations of Europe. Unlike its Slavic sister nations (Poland, Yugoslavia, Russia), Czechoslovakia not only evolved a stable, genuine democracy and a taste for moderation and compromise, but showed un-Slavic efficiency in the management of practical affairs.

It had a flourishing agriculture, and its industries, both heavy and light, were modern and thriving. It had an industrious, skilled population that kept both the economic and social plants in excellent repair.

It is significant that even under the oppressive Nazi occupation the Czechs managed to keep their economy in fairly good working order. There was little destruction by war. After Germany's defeat Czechoslovakia was all set to resume its place as a dynamic, democratic European country. The Marshall Plan would have given it the sinews for accelerated growth and modernization.

However, things turned out differently. In 1948 the Communists took possession of Czechoslovakia and cut it off from the free world. Now, 20 years later, the lid has been taken off and the whole world can see what happens to an advanced, dynamic country under Communist rule.

Let me quote the words of a Czech professor spoken recently to Prof. Remak of the University of California at Santa Barbara:

"The system does not work. Understand, I am a Socialist, not a defector. But it does not work. What is lacking, and that is what it all comes down to, is the will to work, and work discipline. Czechoslovakia has become a lethargic nation. Everyone is asleep at the job. Where will it all end?"

Similar words were used by a Czech economist speaking to the American correspondent Anatole Shub: "Millions of people have forgotten how to work, agriculture has been ruined, we have all those useless industries tied to Russia, our good pre-war plants are all run down." In short, 20 years of Communist rule have turned Czechoslovakia into a backward, underdeveloped country.

No one can tell with certitude what the consequences of rapid, drastic liberalization will be. A miracle of recovery? It is probably safer to be pessimistic. The habit of work once lost is not easily recovered. In Britain, the rust of idleness during the great depression has durably impaired the spirit of the populace. The British economy is still held back by a chronic lethargy.

Rapid change toward freedom, like all drastic change, will generate unrest and frustration, and the danger of a countercoup engineered by Russia will remain for some time. It is a situation that calls for an extraordinary leader who will mobilize energies and generate hope and pride.

An afterthought: Suppose Czechoslovakia had not been taken over by Communists in 1948, and had been allowed to have a full share in the miraculous recovery of post-war Western Europe? What would be its situation at present? Would Czechoslovakia be a second Switzerland or Sweden?

There is a chance that a free, thriving Czechoslovakia would at this moment be wracked and convulsed by a student upheaval in the French style, and whipped by the rage of well-fed, bored intellectuals who see affluence and enterprise as symptoms of debasement and dehumanization, and to whom a freewheeling democracy is a society "stupefied by the narcotic of mass culture."

# How Long Does Change Take?

**August 18, 1968**

It is remarkable that in our time of drastic change, all changes have become more difficult. Our world seems to be getting less and less suitable for people who must undergo change.

Never before has the passage from boyhood to manhood been so painful and so beset with explosions. The passage from backwardness to modernity which in the 19th century seemed a natural process is now straining a large part of the world to the breaking point.

The hoped-for-changes from poverty to affluence, from subjugation to equality, and from work to leisure do not enhance social stability but threaten social dissolution.

One begins to wonder whether change is at all possible; whether grown-up people can really change. And here the story of Moses and the Exodus teaches us a sobering lesson. Moses wanted to turn a tribe of enslaved Hebrews into free men. You would think that all he had to do was gather the slaves and tell them that they are free. But Moses knew better.

He knew that the transformation of slaves into free men was more difficult and painful than the transformation of free men into slaves. He knew that the change from slavery to freedom requires many other drastic changes. First a change in environment, a migration from one country to another. Hence the Exodus. More vital was the endowment of the ex-slaves with a new identity and a sense of rebirth. Moses staged the drama of rebirth in the Sinai peninsula. No playwright and no impresario has ever staged such a grandiose drama. The setting had a live volcano, and the cast included the mighty Jehovah himself.

What was the denouement? Moses discovered that no migration, no drama, and no miracles could turn slaves into free men. It cannot be done. So he led the slaves back into the desert, and waited 40 years until the slave generation died, and a new generation, desert born and bred, was ready to enter the promised land.

All revolutionary leaders, though they fervently preach change, know that people cannot change. Unlike Moses they have neither a handy desert nor the patience to wait 40 years. Hence the purges and the terror to get rid of the grown-up generation.

It is of interest that even in the objective world of science man's mind is not more malleable than in the habit-bound world of everyday life. Max Plank[69] maintained that a new scientific truth does not triumph by convincing its opponents, but because its opponents eventually die, and a new generation grows up that is familiar with it. Here, too, you need 40 years in the desert.

---

[69] Max Plank (1858-1947), German physicist and Nobel Prizewinner, who founded quantum theory.

# The Practical Attitude

August 25, 1968

Nowadays we take the practical attitude for granted. We seem to think that there is in most people an inborn inclination to make use of every device and circumstance to facilitate their work and further their ends. Yet far from being natural, the practical sense has been throughout history a rare phenomenon. Its prevalence is a peculiarity of the Occident; and even here it asserted itself only during the last two or three centuries.

From their first appearance, civilizations almost everywhere were preoccupied with the spectacular, the fantastic, the sublime, the absurd, and the playful with hardly a trickle of ingenuity seeping into the practical and useful. Even as late as the 17th century, the view prevailed in the West that there was something profane and indecent in using sublime knowledge for practical ends. A profound cultural and social transformation was necessary before the practical attitude could be accepted as legitimate and desirable.

Writing was first invented in the Near East for a practical purpose, namely, to facilitate accounting in storerooms and treasuries. But from the very beginning the men who practiced the craft of writing were in a category by themselves. The scribe, unlike the smith, carpenter, brewer, potter, and others, did not produce anything tangible and of unquestioned usefulness.

Furthermore, the scribe was from the beginning an adjunct of management rather than a member of the labor force. Inevitably, this special position of the scribe induced in him attitudes and biases that had to have a profound effect on the outlook of any society in which he played a prominent role. His lack of an unequivocal sense of usefulness set his face against practicalness and usefulness as a test of worth.

★

On the whole it seems to be true that where the equivalents of the intellectual constitute a dominant class, there is little likelihood of ingenuity finding wide application in practical affairs. The inventiveness that now and then breaks through in such social orders is usually fanciful, magical, and playful.

Hero's[70] steam engine was used to work tricks in temples and to divert people at banquets. Archimedes[71] looked on his ingenious mechanical inventions as playthings, "the recreation of a geometer at play." In Mandarin-dominated China, the potent inventions of the magnetic compass, gunpowder, and printing hardly affected daily life. The compass was used to find a desirable orientation for graves; gunpowder was used to frighten off evil spirits, and printing was employed mainly to multiply amulets, playing cards, and paper money.

In the Occident, too, the elite of clerks during the Middle Ages and the early humanists during the Renaissance decried revolutionary innovations in the way of doing things. The humanists were hostile to the invention of printing and ignored the great geographical discoveries. The Occident began to assume its present aspect when the diffusion of literacy, a consequence of the introduction of paper and printing, cracked the intellectual's monopoly on education and the management of affairs.

★

---

[70] Hero, demigod of Greek mythology, representing courage and sacrifice.
[71] Archimedes of Syracuse (287BC-21BC), Greek mathematician, inventor, and scientist.

The exceptional prominence given to the practical in America stems partly from the fact that we have here, for the first time in history, a civilization that operates its complex government and economy and satisfies most of its cultural needs without the aid of the typical intellectual. Perhaps the recent realization of the country's dependence, for its defense and progress, on pure science and the performance of scientific theoreticians might presage a lessening of, if not an end to, the cult of the practical. Almost all recent pronouncements in praise of science and scientists have an undertone of depreciation of the merely practical.

It is remarkable that the intellectual's antipathy toward the practical seems to persist even when he is apparently up to his neck in purely practical affairs. In present-day Communist regimes, the dominant intelligentsia are absorbed in the highly practical process of industrializing a vast expanse of the globe's surface, yet their predilection is for the monumental, grandiose, spectacular, and miraculous. It is not at all strange that they should have left the details of housing, food, clothing, sanitation and other components of everyday life in a relatively primitive state.

# The Common People Set to Work

## September 1, 1968

To me it is a miracle that 200 million people who are largely the descendents of rejects and dropouts from Europe should have created in this country the most important material power on the planet. I do not think that our engineers, scientists and technologists are markedly superior to their kind elsewhere, or that our natural resources are vaster or more accessible than anywhere else.

No, America's unprecedented material achievement has its roots not in our natural resources or in the performance of a group of exceptionally endowed individuals, but in what has happened here to common people. Never since the beginning of time have the masses had a chance to show what they can do on their awn.

I remember Charlie Sorenson's[72] shrewd report of what he had seen in Leningrad in the 1920s. He found that in the higher fields of engineering, like turbine building, the Russians were doing a pretty good job, but anything that had to be done by common people was in an awful mess. This was 40 years ago, and it is still so today.

Sorenson's conclusion was that we need not worry about Russia catching up with us as long as the common people are kept under the thumb of commissars. When you think of the marvels of food production achieved by Russian farmers on their tiny private plots of ground, and of the unmatched ingenuity displayed by Russian blackmarketeers, you'll realize what a release of boundless energy would take place if the Russian people were told to

---

[72] Charles Emil Sorenson (1881-1968), American Vice-Chair of the Ford Motor Company until 1950.

come and get it the way this country told the millions of immigrants from Europe.

Soviet Russia knows how to foster the exceptional skills requisite for the manufacture of complex machinery and instruments, even the harnessing of the atom and launching of Sputniks. But it seems helpless in anything which requires an automatic readiness of the masses to work, day in, day out.

To a degree this holds true even of Britain. There, too, scientists and top technicians perform uncommonly well, but the mass of people see no reason to bestir themselves.

# The Russian Mindset

## September 8, 1968

Zinaida Shokovskay is a Russian princess brought up in France and married to a Frenchman. She visited Moscow in 1957 and wrote a book, *The Privilege Is Mine*. Her writing is delightful—lucid, precise, civilized. Her book crystallized in my mind something I have known for a long time. The change in Russia has been, not mainly ideological, political nor economic, but biological.

Stalin liquidated the most civilized segment of the Russian population and made of Russia a nation of lower mujicks.[73] Most of the city-bred Russians were killed off, imprisoned or exiled. She searched the faces in the street of Moscow: "It was hopeless trying to find one single face which clearly belonged to a born city dweller."

You get the impression that the suspicion and the rudeness which manifest themselves in Russia's foreign dealings are a reflection of this suspicion and rudeness which permeate the lives of the people, high and low. In Russia "even the most commonplace activities assume a sinister air of secrecy."

What she holds against the Soviet government is not that it has not been able to provide the citizens of such a rich country with good life but "the fear which rules men's lives in Russia today." The fear, she thinks, is more degrading than hunger and cold, and is a sign of something rotten within the regime.

---

[73] mujicks is a term used for, typically Russian, peasants.

Now, Soviet Russia is undoubtedly a going concern with an air of permanence. It does not operate smoothly and efficiently, but it manages to feed, clothe, house, and educate its minions. She was aware of an "all-pervading atmosphere of discontent" and of "a clear division between government and people, as if the latter were making a point of dissociating themselves from the former."

But my feeling is that the attitudes and practices of the Soviet government reflect to a considerable extent attitudes and beliefs indigenous to a nation made up of lower mujicks. It is probably true that in thinking of Russia one ought not to confuse the victims with the executioners. But it is also true that the two have an awful lot in common.

One thing is certain: the Russians are not going to revolt; they will not do a Czechoslovakia. If drastic change takes place in Russia it will come from above. Despite, their education, the Russians are still as submissive as Lenin[74] knew them, "so patient, so accustomed to privation."

---

[74] Lenin, Vladimir (1870-1924), Russian Marxist revolutionary and creator of the Soviet Communist Party.

# The Middle Class Under Siege

## September 22, 1968

The other Sunday I watched Negroes going to church. They were well-dressed and prosperous looking—typical middle class. It occurred to me that the real "international" is that of the middle class. Workers are and look different in different countries despite all the talk of a "workers' international." The same is true of aristocrats, intellectuals and other human types. But the typical middle class family looks the same in Tokyo, Timbuktu or even in Moscow.

One has the feeling that what we know as "modern times" is closely bound up with the middle-class pattern. Domination by aristocrats, intellectuals, workers or soldiers will always manifest a return to past eras—to feudalism, the Middle Ages, or even the ancient river-valley regimes of Egypt and Mesopotamia.

Without, a genuine middle class there would have been neither capitalism nor the industrial revolution, nor any other revolution. Most revolutionary leaders come from the middle class. Add the fact that most of the writers, artists, scientists and inventors come from the same class and it becomes obvious that modem western civilization is largely the creation of the middle class.

Yet when we try to explain why capitalism and industrialism did not develop in China and India or in Poland and Spain we hardly ever point to the fact that none of these countries had a genuine middle class living in self-governing cities.

Is it possible to have a freewheeling science, literature and art, or even an effectively functioning modern city, without a middle class? At its best, a Communist revolution is a Caesarian operation to give birth to an industrial society in a country without a middle class.

The 19th century was the century of the middle class par excellence. It is true that the middle class was making headway for centuries, but up to the 19th century it was the aristocracy that set the tone and shaped events. During the 19th century the middle class imposed its rules and tastes not only on the marketplace but on the other spheres of life. It was a Victoria[75] with middle class views and attitudes who gave the name to the century.

In the second half of the 20th century the middle class finds itself battered and beleaguered, and fighting for its very existence. It has been extirpated in a sixth of the globe by genocidal Communists and is on the defensive in most other countries. In America, just now the middle class is pressed hard by an alliance of enraged intellectuals, hoodlum students, and Black Power murder boys.

Can the middle class go on doing business as usual and survive? The public is being persuaded that self-defense is an over-reaction which runs counter to democratic procedure; that to strike out against those who bully us and box our ears would be vigilant-ism if not fascism. The same people also decry the police as blue fascists. We are told to keep cool, conciliate our enemies, and act like good Christians.

My feeling is that the more the militant minorities are con-vinced that the middle class will not strike back, the more fervent will be their zeal to besmirch and shred the social fabric. The sight of a tame enemy incites them to a most reckless ferocity.

---

[75] Refers to the era marked by Queen Victoria's reign from 1837 to 1901.

# Today's Prophets

There has been a gradual narrowing of the range of predictability during the past 500 years. In the heyday of Christianity predictability reached the utmost limit—the life beyond. In the era which followed the idea of progress took the place of millennial prognostication, and the range of predictability was narrowed down a century or so.

With the end of the First World War predictability shrunk further; the craving for security took the place of hope, and people were satisfied if they could foresee the course of a single lifetime. If the shrinking continues we shall be satisfied if we can predict in the evening the eventualities of next morning.

Such a shrinking has already occurred in some totalitarian countries where a man considers himself fortunate if he can be certain that he will not be imprisoned, exiled or liquidated between going to bed and getting up.

It sometimes seems that it is with predictability as it is with wealth: There is so much of it in a society, and when one person has most of it there is little left for everybody else. When a Stalin can predict the future because he has the power to make his predictions come true, the life of the average man becomes unpredictable.

It also seems that the closer we are to the future the less we know about it.

In the past, societies with a vivid conception of the life beyond were indifferent to prognostication, divination, and prophecy. The ancient Egyptians who expended much treasure and effort in

**87**

preparing for the hereafter did not develop any sort of astrology, while the Babylonians who had no faith in a hereafter cultivated divination.

Hebrew prophecy was at its height when resurrection was not as yet an article of faith. In Europe, astrology came into prominence during the Renaissance when millennial Christianity lost its hold on the educated. It strikes us as strange that the religiously emancipated Frederick the Second should have been addicted to astrology.

Our present addiction to pollsters and forecasters is a symptom of our chronic uncertainty about the future. Even when the forecasts prove wrong we still go on asking for them. We watch our experts read the entrails of statistical tables and graphs the way the ancients watched their soothsayers read the entrails of a chicken.

# Tomorrow Has Become a Dirty Word

## October 13, 1968

One can hardly exaggerate the role of misplaced persons—immigrants, exiles, outcasts, misfits—in human development.

It is well to remember that, compared with other animals, man is a misfit on this planet. He lacks the inborn skills and specialized organs which make other animals accomplished specialists, admirably adapted to their environment. It was the effort to finish himself, to fit into and master an inhospitable world, that released man's creative energies and made him uniquely human.

Misplacement induces a tendency toward overstepping, initiating, and innovating. In a stagnant society every individual fits the slot he is born into. The dynamism of a modern society is partly the result of a sharp increase in individual misplacement.

It is only the few who know their life's work from the beginning. In most cases people stumble into careers and many of them spend their lives striving for a milieu befitting their natural bent. This striving releases a copious flow of energies, and manifests itself in a ferment of innovation.

There is one category of misfits which constitutes a chronic threat to social stability; namely, the adolescents who have to fit into the adult world. No country is a good country for its juveniles, and even in normal times every society is in the grip of a crisis when a new generation passes from boyhood to manhood.

The juvenile's self-consciousness robs him of his genuineness, while his penchant for self-dramatization prompts him to extremist poses and gestures. In his restless groping for an identity he will join any mass movement and plunge into any form of spectacular action.

Adolescents become sheer mischief makers when their entrance into the adult world is delayed or when they simply refuse to grow up. Right now our society is strained to the breaking point by juveniles who insist that the adult world must be totally transformed to suit their needs and tastes.

In a time of rapid, drastic change there is apparently no room for wailing, for apprenticeship, and for persistent effort. We want to leap rather than grow. Thus impatience has become the chief trait which characterizes the temper of our times. The future is now, and hope has turned into desire. This is particularly true in an affluent, permissive society. Tomorrow has become a dirty word.

# The Destructive Rush for Happiness

## October 20, 1968

There is a fact that stares us in the face but which we refuse to see; the inverse relation between grievance and protest. The less justified the grievance the more violent the protest. Where the wrong is tangible and obvious the protest will be limited and specific. It is when the wrong is vague or even fictitious that the protest is likely to become revolutionary, to be directed against the Establishment, the power structure, and the whole way of life of a society.

In the San Francisco Bay area the ugliest student protest erupted at San Francisco State College where the administration was responsive to student needs and tried its utmost to satisfy them. The most violent Negro riots occurred in cities like Detroit and New Haven where mayors and city governments were particularly sympathetic to the Negro, and zealous in righting his wrongs.

It is sheer obtuseness to maintain that riots will cease once Negroes and students are given everything they ask for, The opposite seems to be true. President Summerskill of San Francisco State sided with the militant students against his own administration. He was as noble a paper tiger as any Maoist could hope to lay his hands on, and they chased him off the campus. It has been proven again and again that tame enemies and tame battlegrounds constitute an ideal milieu for riots.

It is true that a just society must strive with all its might to right every wrong even if righting wrongs is a highly perilous undertaking. But, if it is to survive, a just society must be strong and resolute enough to deal with those who mistake its goodwill for weakness.

It has been so in the past, but it is much more so now: The time when dreams are realized and hopes fulfilled is a time of trouble. The danger is always great that when we try to realize a dream it may turn into a nightmare.

Who would have dreamt that an unprecedented improvement in the lot of the Negro would result in burned and looted cities, that the unprecedented affluence of the young would bring into being adolescent skid rows with adolescent whores, pimps, dope peddlers, moochers, and derelicts, and a mirthless, perpetual masquerade that unprecedented opportunities for education would bring anarchy to places of learning?

Our time is seeing a revolution against striving and effort. There is a clamor for instant manhood, instant power, instant cash, and instant happiness.

# The Usefulness of Play

## October 27, 1968

It is a fact that retarded children who can barely read and write learn readily to paint, model in clay, and make mosaics of appealing beauty.

Similarly, the Australian aborigines who had not domesticated an animal or a plant and went through millennia without pottery, weaving, metallurgy, etc., have bark paintings of singular beauty.

The old stone age hunters who lived 30,000 years ago in France and northern Spain had only the most rudimentary weapons and tools, yet the murals of animals they painted in the caves of Altamira and Lascaux are masterpieces unsurpassed by any age.

These facts indicate that art is far more ancient than any utilitarian practice or device. No matter what the prehistorians may tell us about the struggles and tribulations of earliest man, we have ample evidence that he had not only the impulse but the leisure to create things of beauty which were not immediately and vitally essential to his survival.

This passionate preoccupation with the non-essential and superfluous—this lightheartedness—is the most striking ingredient of man's uniqueness. All other forms of life are deadly serious and purposeful. Man alone toys, tinkers, and experiments to no useful purpose.

The beauty of it is that, eventually, man's playful, purposeless tinkering resulted in useful devices.

All through the ages man's inventiveness was greatest when he played and tinkered with things at leisure and to no useful purpose.

Thus it is true to say that play has been man's most useful occupation.

The fact that man survived and became what he is, not because he was more purposeful, practical and hardworking than other creatures, but because of his creative playfulness, has a special relevance in an affluent age. Spreading affluence may release destructive forces by blurring the individual's sense of purpose and usefulness, and inducing a fervent groping for substitutes to replace lost values. Might not creative tinkering canalize the destructive forces?

People with a vivid sense of growth are not overly concerned with purpose and usefulness, and are not likely to plunge into a desperate search for new values.

# The "Stupid American" Myth

### November 3, 1968

It seems vitally important to professional intellectuals everywhere to believe that Americans are stupid. We are told that we are too stupid to have an intelligent foreign policy; too stupid to solve the problems of our cities; too stupid to manage our affairs in general.

How, then, did we build this country? How did we manage to tame a savage continent in an incredibly short time and turn it into a cornucopia of plenty? How did we, the dropouts of Europe, build in this continent the greatest material power?

The intellectual will never forgive us that we built America without their guidance; that in this country common people do things which in other countries are done only by elites.

When you compare what common, ignorant people have done on this continent with what the intellectuals are doing in the Communist countries, you cannot avoid the conclusion that the intellectuals are a bloody nuisance. In Russia the intellectuals had to kill 30 million men, women and children in order to build a few factories and dams. On this continent we welcomed 30 million immigrants from Europe and together built our factories and dams.

Of late the self-styled intellectuals have discovered that we are not only stupid but also corrupt and dehumanized. They speak of America as "a great death continent populated only with machines and walking corpses." They say that in mastering a savage continent we were "only intent on sucking all vitality, and the creative instinct of the universe in order to foster with them, the leveling power of dead matter, and a swarm of automatic ghouls."

The quotations are from France. But you can hear, an echo of this ponderous double-talk in the utterances of some of our enraged intellectuals, and in the doctrinaire baby talk of some campus hoodlums of the SDS (Which should be renamed "Students for a Non-Democratic Society").

There is evidence on every hand that the intellectuals are not fit to rule, that they are unfit to create and run a free society, and that with all their knowledge and expertise they cannot create and operate an economy of plenty.

We must tell this fact to common people everywhere—in Europe, in Asia, in Africa, and in Latin America. There is an America buried in the soil of every country and the soul of every people, but only the common people can unearth and discover it.

# Avant-Garde Usefulness

## November 10, 1968

They have been predicting the dire things that would happen to art, literature, and culture in general if the lowbrow masses assert themselves and impose their tastes on a society. But could anything equal the inanity and puerility spewed at present by avant-garde cliques and by highbrow guardians of our culture?

Yet more significant than the fact that at present poets write abstrusely, painters paint abstractly, and composers impose unintelligible music in the presence of a receptive audience, of people ready to admire what they cannot understand—ready to pay hard cash for that which has no meaning on principle.

Total innovation is the refuge of the innately clumsy and untalented; it offers them a situation where their ineptness is acceptable and natural.

The beauty of it is that, with all their ineptness and even fraudulence, the avant-garde innovators have a vital role to play.

The avant-garde, counteract this deadening influence, and fulfill the vital role of keeping the gates open to the few real talents who will eventually sweep away the inanities of the experimenters, and build the new with a sure hand. This is already taking place here and there.

In San Francisco at Gumps, you can see canvasses by Bryan Wilson and you realize what a true talent can make of abstract painting. Here is the painting of a meadow. The grass is just a splash of pure green, the trees in the background a mere smear, a brownish fence that is not a fence cuts across the field patches of white and chocolate represent cows, and light somehow filters through a gap in the row of trees.

Never before have I had so tangible an impression of the lushness of grass. You realize that a realistic rendering of grass, trees, fence, cows, light and sky would have greatly detracted from, or even destroyed, the living feeling of lushness. You suddenly have an inkling of what abstract painting strives for and can achieve.

# Minority Anti-Semitism

## November 17, 1968

The Black Power murder boys are siding with the Arabs against Israel. Yet a U.N. report estimates that in Southern Sudan the Arabs have killed more than a half million Negroes between 1963 and 1966. An equal number were driven from their villages and are wandering in the brush as refugees, hunted by government troops. A report in the *New York Times* early this year showed that in 1968 conditions in the south of Sudan were, if anything, getting worse.

It is questionable whether intensified Negro anti-Semitism has anything to do with the presence of Jewish shopkeepers in the ghettos. The anti-Semitism of the Negro intellectuals is more virulent than that of common Negroes who buy in Jewish stores. No, the Negro's hostility toward the Jews is an hostility toward a challenge and a reproach.

The Jews make the Negro uncomfortable. The trouble is that although both Negroes and Jews have memories of oppression and discrimination (the word ghetto originally denoted the segregated Jewish quarter in a European city) they are as diametrically opposed as two human types can be.

The city has been an optimal milieu for the Jews, and a slough of despond for the Negroes. The city is the greatest opportunity and the worst influence. To thrive in the city one must have ambition and persistence to make the most of its opportunities, and discipline to resist temptation. The Negro has neither.

The Jewish example shows what persistent, patient striving and a passion for education can do for a man in this country even in the teeth of discrimination. This is a fact which the Negro vehemently rejects. It sticks in his gullet. The Jew impairs the authenticity of the Negro's grievances and alibis. He threatens the Negro's most precious possession: the freedom to fail.

Then there is Israel. Think of it: A few thousand Jews, some of them fugitives from Hitler's gas chambers, rebuild and modernize a backward, neglected country. They make the desert bloom like a garden; they convert shopkeepers into workers and soldiers; and last year they defeated three Arab armies in six days.

Here again you have a miracle achieved by hard, ceaseless striving, total dedication, patient organization—things that are anathema to the Negro. And who can doubt that had the Arabs defeated Israel and wiped it off the face of the earth, there would have been a sense of relief, even of elation, in the breast of every Negro leader.

Since the Israelis won the war, the Black power boys are foaming at the mouth about "the Middle East murderers of colored people."

# Intellectual Restlessness

## November 24, 1968

One could perhaps have predicted that a loss of Empire would promote the socialization of Britain.

The Empire provided prestigious employment for a considerable portion of the educated classes. It would, therefore, have been reasonable to foresee that potential colonial administrators without adequate employment would favor a managed social order run by their kind.

Socialization as a substitute for Empire! One might almost say that a socialist Britain governed by intellectuals is a form of colonialism. The difference between colonialism by capitalists and colonialism by intellectuals is that colonialism by intellectuals begins at home.

It is fascinating to observe how much more the end of Empire has affected the British intellectuals, who liked to pose as anti-imperialist, then the aristocrats and businessmen who were supposedly the chief beneficiaries of imperial rule.

One wonders how much of "the unbought grace of life" of the British intellectuals derived from the fact that British red covered half of the map of the world. They have seen this map from childhood and no amount of anti-imperialist patter could blur the axiom they knew—that the British were born rulers.

There are at present British intellectuals hanging on to teaching jobs in Malaya, Borneo and other out-of-the-way places, who speak of the vanished Empire in mystical terms. They call it "a modern majadesha (middle-kingdom)", with its gates at Singapore, and its residents in Tibet and Gilgit.

They blame America for destroying Britain's pride in its empire by having propagated the belief that imperial power was exercised wickedly. The British intellectual finds the atmosphere of a diminished Britain stifling. He hungers for grandeur and lordship.

Now, the predicament of the British intellectual is also the predicament of most European intellectuals. They need something powerful and impressive to identify themselves with. But since the end of World War II nation, race and social millennium have lost their appeal as objects of identification.

Nationalist and racialist slogans sound hollow in post-Hitlerian Europe; and after Stalin the dream of a heaven on earth seems a prelude to a nightmare.

There is left only one potent source of pride—a United Europe. To both British and continental intellectuals it will seem a liberation when they can take their minds off the prospects of a diminished and lusterless fatherland or the tired slogans of a millennium, and contemplate the potentialities of a fabulous sub-continent, beautiful and powerful, possessed of more talent, skill and learning than any other part of the world, and with a history unequalled in brilliance and achievement.

The chief lesson of the present explosion in France is that national aggrandizement can no longer be a source of mass enthusiasm.

# The Social Surgeon

December 1, 1968

Our social doctors are speaking about the social body as if it were a real body.

Listen: "It is a most dangerous error to treat symptoms and not get at the root causes of the disease itself." This is a sociologist talking about riots and crime in the streets. Just to stop the rioters and the muggers is "to treat symptoms." Society is sick and these social doctors say that we have to cure the whole of a society—send every soul to the cleaners before the riots and the mugging can be really stopped.

Now the simple fact is that society is not a body, and sociologists are not doctors, and the talk about the root causes of the disease, the underlying infection, etc., is pretentious double talk.

It is probably true that in human affairs there are no deep causes—there are no depths, only surface and symptoms. When you see the role example and imitation play in shaping events, and how minds are affected by words, gestures and symbols, you realize that history is made by trivial, superficial agencies; by gimmicks and toys. Not to know that in human affairs the trivial is not trivial is to ignore a chief ingredient of man's uniqueness.

It is man's superficiality that makes him so fantastic a creature. His nobleness and vileness, his hatreds, loves and dedications are all skin-deep. The sudden, drastic transformations of which he is capable are due to the fact that the tensions which shape his attitudes are surface phenomena.

Think of the incredible transformations we have witnessed in recent decades. In less than 20 years the Japanese and the Germans have become the foremost traders of the world, and the Jews the foremost warriors.

When solving human problems we have to grasp, and hang on to, what we see. Riots, mugging and crime in the streets should be dealt with not as if they were the outer manifestations of some dark disorders in the cellars of the mind, but as the perverse high jinks and shenanigans of spoiled, unruly juveniles of every age who think they can get away with it. You have here a virulent form of juvenile delinquency on a large scale. Swift, unrelenting justice will take the fun out of lawlessness and cause juveniles to think twice before they let themselves go.

There is no proof that righting wrongs and satisfying demands can stop riots and crime. It has been proven again and again that tame, meek antagonists incite juveniles to violence. Both the hoodlum students and the Black Power murder boys have displayed their utmost savagery on campuses and in cities where authority was hesitant, unprepared and genuinely benevolent.

What can social psychologists and sociologists prescribe for well fed, well clad Negro juveniles who want to have a ball looting, burning and shooting, and for students who want to make history on the campuses? What sort of soul healing is there for a student leader at Columbia who is reported to have said: "As much as we would like to, we are not strong enough as yet to destroy the United States. But we are strong enough to destroy Columbia!"

# Intellectual Contempt for Man

December 8, 1968

The history of the intellectual begins with the invention of writing in the Middle East about 3000 BC. No other human type displayed its peculiar characteristics so fully and clearly at its first appearance. The earliest scribe had already the essential earmarks of the latest model intellectual.

Writing was invented as a device of bookkeeping—to keep track of the intake and outgo of warehouses and treasuries. The scribe was one of the craftsmen attached to the temples and royal households. But from the very beginning the scribe was in a category by himself. Unlike the carpenter, smith, weaver, brewer, etc., the scribe did not produce anything tangible and of unquestioned utility.

From his first appearance the intellectual was without an automatic and unequivocal sense of usefulness.

Secondly, unlike the other craftsmen the scribe was a member of the supervisory rather than of the working force. In the tomb paintings of Egypt and on the clay tablets of Mesopotamia the scribe is pictured standing alongside the overseer with his whip, both facing the common people who did the world's work and paid the taxes.

From his first appearance the intellectual was aware of his superior status, and his birthright to supervise, direct, and ride the illiterate masses.

All through history the intellectual has hankered for a return of the golden age of the scribe-dominated civilizations of ancient Egypt and Mesopotamia. One not should be surprised to hear the

Irish poet, W. B. Yeats[76], urge "the despotic rule of the educated classes" or the Scottish poet, MacDiarmid[77], sing the praises of Soviet Russia for its "mental spa"—rule by an elite of intellectuals.

The intellectual feels at home only in an aristocratic milieu, where an exclusive elite is in charge of affairs. He would prefer an elite that is literate, but will put up with one that is not. What he cannot endure is a society dominated by common people. There is nothing he loathes more than government of and by the people.

Contempt for common folk is an ingredient present in the make-up of even the most noble intellectuals. Here is what Emerson[78] thought of the masses: They are "rude, lame, unmade, pernicious in their demands and influence, and need not to be flattered but to be schooled. I wish not to concede anything to them but to tame, drill, divide am break them up and make individuals out of them... If government knew how, I should like to see it check, not multiply, the population."

---

[76] William Butler Yeats (1865-1939), Irish poet and dramatist.
[77] Hugh MacDiarmid (1892-1978), Scottish poet and self-styled communist.
[78] Ralph Waldo Emerson (1803-1882), American poet and essayist.

# The Danger of Affluence

December 15, 1968

Freedom is freedom from nature—from the iron necessities and the implacable determinism which dominate nature.

It was nature's niggardliness, its failure to give him inborn skills and specialized organs to serve him as weapons and tools, that forced man to finish himself by technology, and thereby free himself from the animal imprisonment of nature.

The significant point is that nature is not only around us but also within us. The contest with nature goes on on two fronts, and victory over the nature that is around us does not free us from the tyranny of the instincts, the anxieties, the lusts, the savage impulses, and the dark, destructive forces which lie in wait in the cellars of our mind.

Indeed, not only are the two fronts not dovetailed and coordinated, but victory on one front is usually followed by defeat on the other front. In our time, the unprecedented triumphs of the technician and the scientist have set the stage for the psychiatrist. On the other hand, the complete control over the body and mind by a population of yogis and ascetics usually results in economic stagnation and decay.

We are only now beginning to get an inkling of the dangers and tribulations of affluence. The freedom we gain by mastering nature around us may become destructive when we do not know what do with it.

The dark, destructive forces released by affluence can serve to fuel the creative process. Where there is no growth affluence brings frustration, boredom, strife, lust for power.

We know that affluence threatens the young—in particular since it brings about a condition of delayed manhood. It is difficult for the young to grow up and prove their manhood in an effortless society. Hence juvenile delinquency in its virulent form of rioting is becoming the hallmark of an affluent age.

Freedom and power are among the crucial opposite of man's existence. The desire for freedom is the attribute of a "have-not" type of self. Those who lack the capacity or temperament to achieve much in an atmosphere of freedom usually will clamor for power.

# Who Are the Sick Americans?

December 22, 1968

Some time ago a professor of mathematics in one of our larger universities sent me the reprint of a lecture on the future of science which he had delivered in Japan while there on a Fulbright fellowship.

As I turned the pages of the pamphlet I came upon a paragraph in which the professor told his audience of Japanese scientists what America is like. America, said the professor, is a country without friendship and neighborliness, a social wasteland charged with suspicion, envy, and malice.

I did not know what to think. The letter that came with the pamphlet was written by an intelligent, sensitive person who is easily alarmed. He had read something I had written on the relation between man and nature and was disturbed by my cocky attitude toward nature.

The writer of the letter was not the type of person who would willfully slander his own country before an audience of foreigners. What he wrote about America expressed something he had experienced and observed, something that had eaten into his mind and darkened his view.

It suddenly dawned on me that what the professor described so vehemently was not America but the department of mathematics at his university. Though I had no particular information about mathematicians and departments of mathematics, I knew from reading of the soul-wrenchlng tensions and the suspicion and malice which are likely to pervade whenever men who deal with words and symbols congregate.

Contrary to what one would expect, the vying for intangibles such as "recognition," renown and prestige is usually more vicious and pitiless than the striving for money and possessions. The real rat race is in the realm of the immaterial.

Here is how Somerset Maugham[79] describes the life of the intellectuals in Paris: "It is a merciless conflict in which one gives violent battle to another, in which one clique attacks another clique, in which you must always be on guard against the guns and snares of your enemies, and in which, indeed, you can never be quite sure that a friend will not knife you in the back."

My sensitive professor was obviously not built for cutthroat competition and he had projected the infighting, backbiting, mistrust and ill will which surrounded him upon us. He was an unhappy, sick man and he blamed us for his misery.

---

[79] Somerset Maugham (1874-1965), English playwright and novelist.

# False Clichés About Americans

## December 29, 1968

It is remarkable how the clichés about America, which most people accept as unquestionably true, usually fail to hold up when tested against the realities of American life.

Americans, we are told, are always on the run and never pause. The fact is that you hardly ever see Americans run when you watch them do the world's work on the docks, in the fields, on construction sites, in the woods or in factories. The American at work is cool, calm and collected. Sure of his skill, the American goes leisurely about his job, and accomplishes much though he works as if at play.

It is the unskilled, clumsy worker who attacks his work as if he were saving the world, and he must do so if he is to get anything done at all. The uniqueness of America is that it accomplishes the momentous in an unmomentous, prosaic way. It is the mark of a healthy society that it can function well at room temperature.

Again we are told that Americans lack patience—that they are not good for the long haul. Actually the American is wonderfully patient in the preparatory, organizing phase of an undertaking. Whether it be the preparatory work for a building, a production line or an army, the work proceeds so unhurriedly that the onlooker begins to wonder whether anything is going on at all.

The American is aware of the preparatory work not as a preliminary to but as the root of an achievement. With the root firmly anchored and fully functioning, growth proceeds smoothly and almost effortlessly. Buildings shoot up a story a day, ships are discharged and loaded in an incredibly short time.

The cliché is that Americans worship the almighty dollar. Yet in no other society do people spend or give money away so readily. It has always amused me that the radicals in our union are more money conscious than the low-down nondoctrinaire longshoremen.

Finally, we are told that in America everybody is for himself. Here again the cliché comes up against the fact that in no society do people cooperate and help each other so readily as in America. There is far more spontaneous cooperation in self-seeking America than in any socialist or Communist society,

# The Decade of the Young

January 5, 1969

If you want to know whose age we are living in find out who it is that wants to make history.

There was a time in this country when the masses felt they were making history. They plunged into the unknown, cleared the land, built cities, founded states, and propagated new faiths.

After the Civil War businessmen and industrialists thought they had their hands on the steering wheel of history; that, like the builders of the tower of Babel, "nothing will be restrained from them which they have imagined to do."

During the first half of this century politicians like Teddy Roosevelt, Wilson, F.D.R., and Truman came into their own as history makers.

But right now neither the masses nor the industrialists nor the politicians want to make history. They would be happy if history were something that happens to other people, preferably their enemies. Nowadays it is the young, particularly students, who itch to make history.

★

Whether we like it or not, the 1960's will go down as the decade of the young. High school and university students in Indonesia toppled Sukarno and set in motion the liquidation of the second largest Communist party in the world. This incredible and unprecedented event so stunned Mao Tse-tung that he set out to corral the young of China and incite them to turn China upside

**113**

down in Mao's name. This is a Chinese way of securing the allegiance of the young.

In Eastern Europe students are cracking monolithic Communist regimes; and De Gaulle's France was shaken to its foundations by a student uprising. In this country students had a hand in changing our Vietnam policy.

It is difficult to say how effective and durable the present history-making rule of the students is likely to be. In the past, student intrusion into the historic process was episodic, without lasting effects. This was true of student activities in France and Germany after the fall of Napoleon, and of the student uprisings in many European countries during the 1840's. However, in an age of rapid, drastic change student militancy and violence may become a fixed feature of the American style of life.

It is of considerable interest that in this country student unrest had its inception in the civil rights movement. Almost all the student leaders had their first taste of history making on the picket lines of CORE and related Negro organizations. For all we know the most revolutionary consequences of the Negro revolution will be not radical changes in the existence of the Negro, but its effects on white students and juveniles.

Here is an instance of the unfamiliar truth that the most important revolutions are those other people make for us. The French Revolution altered France relatively little, but it created a new Germany. Similarly the consequences of the Russian Revolution will be a United Europe and a new China.

# Idealist Fear the Common Man

## January 12, 1969

The idealists have discovered a new monster: the common man. They tell you it was the common man who ran Hitler's gas chambers, executed Stalin's purges, and is just now committing American atrocities in Vietnam. Let me quote: "It is the man who wants to do his best for his wife and children, keep up the mortgage and buy a new car—it is this man who also releases gas in the chambers and who makes napalm containers."

When, after the assassination of Sen. Robert Kennedy[80] by the Jordanian Sirhan[81], Prof. Arthur Schlesinger Jr.[82] declared that Americans are "the most frightening people in the world," he meant that the average lawnmowing, car-washing, moon-lighting American is potentially a monster.

You ask yourself: Whose age is it that we are living in? Is it the age of the common man? Actually our present age is shaped and dominated by idealists. No other age has seen so vast an expulsion of practical people from the seats of power and their replacement by idealists.

The greatest surprise of the 20th century was sprung when idealists came to power. We believed that money was the root of all evil, that it was the money-grubbing middle class that debased all values, and that mankind's ills would be cured when pure-hearted, selfless idealists took charge of affairs. We were wholly

---

[80] Robert Francis Kenney (1925-1968), American senator who was assassinated while running for the U.S. Presidency.

[81] Sirhan Sirhan (1944- ), Palestinian who assassinated Robert Kennedy.

[82] Arthur Schlesinger Jr. (1917-2007), American historian and social critic.

115

unprepared for the wholesale murder and destruction, the genocide of classes and races, the unimagined suffering brought upon the world when idealists get the power to make their dreams come true.

Go to any country where the soul brothers of our New Left are in power and you will see what there is in store for us if our noble, self-denying, pure-hearted, dedicated idealists ever achieve what they are fighting for.

Sometimes when I listen to the New Left's denunciations of the status quo, and the enumeration of the evils which degrade our life, I have the feeling that I am actually hearing a description of the shape of things to come when the idealists will have realized their dreams.

Over a hundred years ago the Russian Idealist Alexander Herzen, exiled from his homeland, described thus the evils he saw in Western Europe: "There is no regard for law, no justice, not even a semblance of liberty. A secular inquisition reigns supreme... There is only one moral force that still has authority over men, and still demands and receives their obedience and that is fear which is universal."

This surely is a prophetic forecast of what actually came into existence a hundred years later when the idealists in Russia and elsewhere made their dreams come true.

# Jews Must Brace for Worst

**January 12, 1969**

The condemnation of Israel in the U.N. Security Council was the culmination of a tendency which has been shaping up for some time.

There has been an ill wind blowing for Israel. You feel its bite every time you open a newspaper. Dispatches, editorials, letters to the editor presage vaguely a shift in Washington's policy from Israel to the Arabs. Something similar is going on in Britain and in France. Ernest Bevin's[83] algebra is again in vogue: "It pays better to be friends with 200 million Arabs than with 200,000 Jews, to say nothing of the oil."

When the democracies are at a low ebb, as they are now, they are capable of every fatuity. They make the wrong decisions, choose the wrong men, and are unable to recognize their enemies—they actually prefer them to friends. Promises to Israel are made to be broken; no one hesitates to profit at Israel's expense.

I have never been one of the doom-around-the-corner boys. Indeed, I have always known that our greatest worries are most of the time about things that do not come to pass. But since the Hitler decade there has been one subject on which an alarmist view seemed to me not only legitimate but obligatory. Namely, the fate of the Jews.

I cannot forget the shock I experienced when the best educated country in the Occident, in the full sight of 20th century humanity, declared outcast, and outside the law, the most dynamic and

---

[83] Ernest Bevin (1881-1951), British politician and foreign secretary during the establishment of Israel.

creative segment of its population, submit it to the grossest abuse, and almost deprived it of a livelihood, without rousing the wrath of a single country. Not one country remonstrated Hitler, let alone broke off relations with him. On the contrary, the civilized countries were falling over each other in courting the insolent Nazi rulers.

The German Jews constituted an unequalled aggregate of brains, skills and energies, yet no country opened its gates to welcome them. It is on record that empty Australia was reluctant to accept German Jews because it did not want to import a racial problem.

Equally disturbing is the fact that for many years the Jews in Germany and elsewhere refused to take Hitler and Nazism seriously. They refused to become alarmed. They did not believe that so monstrous and apocalyptic an evil was possible in the heart of Europe and in the 20th century.

My feeling is that for the balance of this century Jewish leaders must cultivate the habit of viewing with alarm and expecting the worst. They must, as the poet counseled, "train for ill and not for good."[84]

---

[84] Alfred Edward Housman (1859-1936), British scholar and poet; quote taken from his poem, "Terence, This Is Stupid Stuff."

# Weakness on Campus

January 26, 1969

It is getting more and more difficult to keep in mind that the turmoil and disruption on the campuses are caused by a small minority. Somehow, one has the impression that the passive majority is putty in the hands of the activist minority. You strain your ears in vain for even a faint rumor or resentment coming from the thousands of students who are prevented by brazen nincompoops from pursuing their studies and finishing their education.

You no longer expect a manifestation of outrage among students who see presidents, chancellors, deans and professors insulted to their faces and reviled with the crudest epithets.

The fact that a large number of draft dodgers are at present holed up on the campus has something to do with the non-belligerence of the majority. I also have a hunch that the majority derives a certain benefit from the strain and the confusion created by the confrontationists.

As things are at present it is doubtful whether the majority can become a factor in restoring order on the campus. The prevailing tone and mood in most universities make it unlikely that students who disagree with the tactics of disruption will get mad enough to speak out, let alone hit out, against the minority that interferes with their education. Nor is it certain that compulsory secret voting on crucial issues would result in a decisive vote against the militants.

The tragic figure on the campus is the administrator. The reestablishment of order hinges on him, and he stands alone, unsupported by either the student body or the sullen self-righteous faculty. The politicians and the public expect him to act promptly and drastically, but he is hindered by the academic prejudice against police, and the slogan of academic freedom.

Everything depends on the administrator's character and style. If America's campuses are to assume their historic role as centers of reason and intellectual pursuit they will need administrators who delight in battle and who know how to proceed promptly and fiercely against those who break the peace.

Since universities are the abode of "men of words," it is imperative that administrators take words seriously. It would be difficult to exaggerate the harm done to universities by the toleration of violent and besmirching expression. Threats, insults, and foul epithets should be dealt with as with aggressive behavior.

It is unsupportable that obscenities and savage behavior should find more acceptance in houses of learning than in the market place.

# Growing Pains of a New Community

## February 2, 1969

The campaign against the police in Negro ghettos which is often supported by moderate Negroes is bearing strange fruit. The police have made themselves scarce in Negro neighborhoods, and as a result Negro juveniles in combination with Negro criminals have instituted something like a reign of terror.

In a central shopping district in Harlem 75% of the stores were burglarized during the first nine months of 1968. Many of the stores are owned by soul brothers. A Negro owned appliance service store has been robbed 14 times in two years. A Negro record store was held up 22 times in 1968. Stores dealing in African articles are robbed as readily. An increasing number of Harlem residents are buying guns to protect their businesses or their homes.

★

We have been told repeatedly that the Negro ghettos are a creation of white racism. Even if we assign all possible blame to white landlords and to white prejudice in housing matters, the fact remains that the tone and quality of life in the ghettos have something to do with Negro attitudes, habits and aptitudes. It has still to be shown whether left to themselves Negroes can shape and maintain a civilized community.

In this hemisphere Haiti is an example of Negro capabilities. There has been no whitey in Haiti for 150 years. Would it be altogether unreasonable to assume that if left wholly to themselves

Negroes would turn Harlem into another Haiti? I can think of a number of Negro leaders who are potential Doc Duvaliers, and the black power loudmouths are the spitting image of Duvalier's murder boys, the Ton Ton Macoutes.

Yet there is a good chance that the above prognostication is totally wrong. The American climate is not favorable for Doc Duvaliers. If Negro businessmen in Harlem succeed in forming a strong association for mutual protection and insurance it could be the beginning of a process of regeneration which may eventually lead to the birth of an orderly, healthy Negro community.

The capacity for community building is widely diffused in this country, and there is no reason why the Negro should be without it. If the present terror in the ghettos prompts responsible Negroes to work together and trust each other, they could go on shaping a viable community with vigorous organs for mutual help and communal achievement.

It is of interest that historically arrangements for mutual protection, such as the stockade and the citadel, were the seed of the first cities.

# Mankind's Affinity with the Stars

### February 9, 1969

Man is an eternal stranger on this planet. From this incurable strangeness stems our uncurable insecurity, our unfulfillable craving for roots, our passion to cover the planet with manmade compounds. It has always seemed to me that only animals and plants feel wholly at home in this world, and that our human uniqueness is diminished the moment we fit in perfectly anywhere on earth and feel that we truly belong.

I like to play with the fancy that some contagion from outer space has been the seed of man. Our passionate preoccupation with heaven, the stars, and a God somewhere in outer space is a homing impulse. We are drawn back to where we came from. Hence to me the exploration of space has an inner logic.

It also tickles me no end that the astronauts are not elite-conscious intellectuals but lowbrow, ordinary Americans. It has been the genius of the average American to achieve the momentous in an unmomentous, matter-of-fact way. If space exploration remains in their keeping they will soon make of it an everyday routine accessible to all.

The intellectuals call this giving of access to the vulgar—vulgarization. What Goethe[85] said of the Germans holds true of intellectuals in general: Their destiny is to make things difficult.

---

[85] Johann Wolfgang von Goethe (1749-1832), German writer, icon of modern literature.

Where the intellectuals are in power prosaic tasks—like planting and harvesting—become Promethean undertakings.

Finally I found it wonderfully fitting that while they circled the moon the astronauts read aloud from the first chapter of Genesis. Some hysterical women of both sexes found the reading improper. But I remembered a favorite passage in Benjamin Franklin's[86] autobiography:

"The people have a saying that God Almighty is Himself a mechanic, the greatest in the universe; and He is respected and admired more for the variety of His handiwork than for the antiquity of His family."

God is the archetypal innovator and creator. Any time we try the untried, turn a dream into reality, overcome insurmountable obstacles we are in some manner sharing God's style. Why should not the astronauts think of Him who "numbered the stars and called them by name, and meted out the heaven with the span." We have it from Einstein[87] that what he wanted most was "to rethink God's thoughts and know how God created the world."

---

[86] Benjamin Franklin (1706-1790), American Founding Father and Renaissance man; his autobiography is *The Private Life of the Late Benjamin Franklin*.
[87] Albert Einstein (1879-1955), German Nobel-prizewinning physicist and modern leader of the field.

# The Definition of an Intellectual

## February 16, 1969

I have been wiping the floor with the intellectuals these many years, blaming them for everything under the sun. Though I have spelled out many times who these intellectuals are, I am still being asked quite often for a definition of the intellectual. Here it is.

My intellectual is a person who feels himself a member of the educated elite with a God-given right to direct and shape events. He need not be well educated or very intelligent. What counts is the feeling of being a member of the educated elite.

What the intellectual wants above all is to be listened to—with deference. He will forgive you everything if you take him seriously, and allow him to instruct you. It is more important to him to be important than to be free, and he would rather be persecuted than ignored.

Typical intellectuals feel oppressed in a democratic society where they are left alone to do as they please and say whatever they please. They call it "'jester's license," and they envy intellectuals in Communist countries who are persecuted by governments that take intellectuals seriously.

The typical intellectual can be over-educated as Toynbee, Sartre[88] and as Hans Morgenthiau[89], or undereducated as Lee

---

[88] Jean-Paul Charles Aymard Sartre (1905-1980), French writer and activist.
[89] Hans Joachim Morgentiau (1904-1980), German-Jewish scholar of international politics.

Oswald[90] and Hitler. I can see raised eyebrows: Oswald and Hitler intellectuals? Yes—typical intellectuals. Lee Oswald's pretensions and absurdities were emblematic of the attitudes and impulses of a self-styled intellectual rather than of a common man.

Does anyone doubt that had Oswald been in Berkeley at the time of the Free Speech Movement he would have become an outstanding leader? He was an illiterate ignoramus, but he considered himself a sophisticated highbrow far above run of the mill Americans.

As to Hitler, he was a genius "man of words" with an unbounded faith in the power of words and ideas. He was driven to action by his own words, by his discovery that he had the power to move people with words. It is doubtful whether a man who does not style himself an intellectual would be overly impressed by his power to move people with words.

The intellectual's feeling that he has a right to make history is an insane delusion. In a Hitler or a Lee Oswald the insanity is patent, but it is present also in normal intellectuals.

The intellectual knows with every fiber of his being that men are not equal, and there are few things he cares for less than a classless society. He is convinced that government is too weighty and complex to be left to common people. He cannot see how anything originating in an uninformed, unprincipled and uncommitted populace could be of any value. There is nothing he loathes more than government by and for the people.

---

[90] Lee Harvey Oswald (1939-1963), American assassin of U.S. President John F. Kennedy; assassinated prior to the formation of a trial.

# Latin-Americanization of the World

## February 23, 1969

Right, now it is, difficult to say whether the advanced countries are influencing the backward, or whether it is the other way around. There has been a change in the tilt of the landscape of hope and faith. Formerly dreams and ideologies flowed from the advanced to the backward countries. Now the flow is in the opposite direction.

The advanced countries are without ardent faith: Their advanced technologies and their know-how enable them to do the momentous in an unimpassioned, prosaic way. Hence those segments of the population in Western Europe and America that are in need of faith can get it principally by an identification with the goings on in Asia, Africa and Latin America.

The heroes of militant students everywhere, and of the black power fanatics in this country, are Mao, Guevara[91] and Castro.[92] It seems to be true that the more technically proficient a society becomes the less capable it is of generating faith. Where there is the necessary skill and equipment to move mountains there is no need for the faith that moves mountains.

Sometimes it seems that in a large part of the world both the political and the intellectual life are being Latin-Americanized. When a general takes over a government, whether in France or in Nigeria, he is following the Latin American pattern. When students take possession of a campus or fight police in the streets they are

---

[91] Che Guevara (1928-1967), Argentine Marxist revolutionary.
[92] Fidel Castro (1926- ), Cuban revolutionary and leader.

echoing and reflecting a style of life fashioned below the Rio Grande.

How true is it that the strong learn more readily from the weak? Most often in history it was the conquerors who learned, willingly from the conquered rather than the other way around. It staggers the mind how little we can do to influence and shape deliberately nations we help and wish well. Our propaganda and expert advice have little effect. Our material aid breeds resentment. And almost everywhere the intellectuals are predisposed to a rabid anti-Americanism.

It is too late in the day for America to try to win anyone with words, and it is even more certain that we cannot win by giving. What then can we do? We can win the world only by example—by making our way of life as good as we know how. Our main problem is not the world but ourselves, and we can win only by overcoming ourselves.

# The Worth of an Average American

March 2, 1969

It has always seemed self-evident to me that a free society is also a skilled society. No matter how free its constitution and laws, a society will not be genuinely free if its people lack technological, social and political skills to do the world's work and manage affairs without tutelage and minute supervision.

It follows that if we want to bring freedom to non-free countries we cannot do it by inculcating a love of freedom, or by having them copy our constitution, but by transmitting to the common people the technological and social expertise which would enable them to do things on their own without masters to shove them around.

I still remember the demonstration I saw some 30 years ago of the diffusion of competence and expertise in this country. It happened during the depression. A construction company had to build a road in the San Bernardino Mountains and the man who was in charge, instead of calling up an employment agency, sent down two trucks to the Los Angeles Skid Row, and anyone who could climb onto the trucks was hired.

When the trucks were full, the drivers put in the tailgates and drove off. They dumped us on the side of a hill in the San Bernardino Mountains, where we found bundles of supplies and equipment. The company had only one man on the spot and he hardly opened his mouth.

We began to sort ourselves out: There were so many carpenters, electricians, mechanics, cooks, men who could handle bulldozers and jackhammers, and even foremen. We put up the tents and the cook shack, fixed latrines and a shower bath, cooked supper, and next morning went out to build the road.

If we had had to write a constitution we probably would have had someone who knew all the whereases and wherefores. We were a shovelful of slime scooped off the pavement of Skid Row, yet we could have built America on the side of a hill in the San Bernardino Mountains.

The man in charge of the construction company obviously knew something about Americans. All through the years, I have kept wondering what sort of man he could have been. Not an intellectual—that's for sure. Not a businessman either. An ex-hobo perhaps? My hunch is he was an army officer. The army knows what Americans are like. I remember reading Gen. Patton's[93] saying: "Never tell an American how to do a thing. Tell him what you want done and he'll surprise you by his ingenuity."

---

[93] George Smith Patton, Jr. (1885-1945), U.S.Army General during WWII.

# The American in Every Man

**March 9, 1969**

Tasks which in other countries are reserved for a select minority, for a specially trained elite, are in this country performed by every Tom, Dick and Harry. Not only did common Americans build and name towns but they also founded states, propagated new faiths, commanded armies, wrote books, and ran for the highest offices. It is this that makes America unprecedentedly new.

It always tickles me to observe how the non-Americanness of the radicals shows itself in their non-egalitarianism. I have yet to meet a radical who truly believes that common people can rule themselves, and can run things without standing leaders. The radical who goes to the masses always goes in search of leadership. In the longshoremen's union the radicals always had a nervous breakdown anytime a common, barely literate longshoreman ran for office and got elected.

To me it seems axiomatic that the common people everywhere are our natural allies and that our chief contribution to the advancement of mankind should be the energizing and activation of lowly folk. We must learn how to impart to common people everywhere the technological, political, and social skills which would enable them, to dispense with the tutorship of the upper classes and the intellectuals. We must deflate the pretensions of self-appointed elites. These elites will hate us no matter what we do, and it is legitimate for us to help dump them into the dustbin of history.

Our foreign aid to the backward countries in Asia, Africa and Latin America should be tailored to the needs of the masses, rather than of the elites. The elites hanker for the trappings of the 20th century. They want steel mills, dams, airlines, skyscrapers, etc. Let them get these trappings from elitist Russia.

Our gift to the masses in the backward countries should be the capacity for self-help. We must show them how to get bread, human dignity, and strength by their own efforts. We must know how to stiffen their backbones so that they will insist on getting their full share of the good life and not allow themselves to be sacrificed to the Moloch[94] of a mythical future.

Let me repeat: There is an America hidden in the soil of every country and in the soul of every people. It is our task to help common people everywhere discover their America at home.

---

[94] Moloch is an ancient Semitic-Phoenician god or general term for "king."

# The Comfortable Alibi of Failure

**March 16, 1969**

The oppressed and injured do have an advantage over the fortunate and the free. They need not grope for a purpose in life nor eat their hearts out over wasted opportunities and unrealized talents. Grievances and extravagant hope are meat and drink to their souls, and there is a hero's garment to fit any size fairytale dreams of the future, and an imperishable alibi to justify individual failure.

How will it fare with the Negro when he has no grievance and no alibi—when he no longer has the freedom to fail?

A good alibi for non-achievement is psychologically more satisfying than an actual achievement. An achievement does not settle anything permanently. We still have to prove our worth anew each day: We have to prove that we are as good today as we were yesterday.

Hemingway wrote several great books. But the glory of past achievements could not make life worth living once Hemingway could no longer write. How much more fortunate and secure the man with a good alibi for not writing a book! He has an alibi for not writing the greatest book, and he is fixed for life.

It is, therefore, safe to predict that the Negro will hold on to the alibi of discrimination as long as he can. One can also predict that the more untenable the alibi becomes the more fervently will the Negro cling to it.

The chief task of the Black Power boys is the preservation of the Negro's alibi. They drum it into the heads of Negro youths that education and effort will not get them anywhere. You see sullen

133

Negro boys and girls sitting bunched together in integrated classes, sneering at anyone who tells them of scholarships waiting for any Negro high school graduate who can read and write well.

The effort put into maintaining and preserving the alibi of discrimination exceeds the effort requisite for the attainment of a most marked achievement.

In Haiti after 150 years of independence the alibi for non-achievement is still alive. You get the same response from people in all walks of life: "I am not capable; it is not my fault." (Pas capable; pas fault moine).

Will the Haitian experience be repeated in this country? Probably not. As freedom and equality become a reality, more and more Negroes will find out that they can hold their own in competition with non-Negroes. To those who "can" the tasks of achievement will be more appealing than strident self-pity.

# Borrowing Progress and Learning

March 23, 1969

It is startling to realize that between 1400 and 1800 A.D. the Eastern influence on the West was far greater than the Western influence on the East. Were it not for the Eastern influence Columbus might not have set out to discover America. And it is well to remember that Asia gave us the instruments—gunpowder, the compass, the astrolabe—with which to subdue it.

It is perhaps true that the vigor of a society shows itself partly in the ability to borrow copiously without ill effects and without losing its identity. A vigorous society has as it were a cast-iron stomach that digests and assimilates anything. The Occident borrowed profusely from other civilizations and thrived on it.

It is a mark of debilitation that at present Asia, Africa, and Latin America are sickening on their borrowings from advanced countries. In Asia only Japan has been vigorous enough to borrow plentifully without getting social indigestion. Early in history Egypt, Crete, India and others borrowed freely from Sumer yet developed unique, vigorous civilizations.

The relation between borrowing and originating is of absorbing interest. One remembers Oscar Wilde's saying: "The true artist is known by the use he makes of what he annexes, and he annexes everything." According to T. S. Eliot "immature poets imitate; mature poets steal."

It is probably true that our originality manifests itself less strikingly in what we originate than in what we do with that which we did not originate. To discover something wholly new can be a matter of chance, of idle tinkering, or even of the chronic dissatisfaction of the untalented.

The Phoenicians invented the alphabet and the Greeks borrowed it from them. Yet how great the discrepancy between what the Phoenicians did with that which they originated, and what the Greeks did with that which they borrowed. And think of the sublime originality displayed by the ancient Hebrews in what they did with the myths they borrowed from Sumer.

The uniqueness of the Occident shows itself most strikingly in the use it made of the magnetic compass and gunpowder it borrowed from China. The Chinese used the compass to find a desirable orientation for graves, and gunpowder to frighten off evil spirits, while the Occident used both to attain world dominion.

There is also the case of the water wheel: The Buddhists used it first to turn prayer wheels—to grind out prayers—while we used it to mill grain.

At bottom the ability to borrow and assimilate is the ability to learn and grow, and it requires a certain degree of confidence. The nonconfident and the overconfident cannot learn: The first feel they cannot grow, while the last feel they need not grow.

# Sputnik and the Misplaced Activists

## March 30, 1969

A university, irrespective of what it teaches, should be a place where talents can be realized, and the individual can grow. Oxford had taught the classics for centuries whereas Cambridge for a long time refused to teach literature and taught mathematics. Yet many more poets came out of Cambridge than out of Oxford.

The complaints of the activist students that our universities do not teach anything about the real world are nonsensical. You learn about the real world not in a university but by going out there and battling the elements.

As you watch the activist students you know beyond doubt that they are first and last not students but men of action—potential organizers and managers. Many of them are intelligent, articulate, even brilliant, but their hunger is not for knowledge and for the mastery of skills, but for action and a taste of power. They would be at home wheeling and dealing on Wall Street.

But a twist of history has landed these potential men of action on the campus, and cast them in the role of dangerous two-bit intellectuals.

It all began with Sputnik, the fateful toy the Russians placed in orbit in 1956. For the first time in its history America found itself left behind, found itself in the humiliating situation of having to catch up with the backward Russians. We reacted hysterically. We set out to produce scientists and technicians wholesale, and diverted a flood of billions into the universities. Energies and ambitions followed.

Thus a toy, a mere gimmick, brought about a change in the tilt of our social landscape, and a change in the direction of flow of social energies. This is the way history is made. And now you have this army of potential wheelers and dealers throwing their weight around on the campus and in literary and artistic cliques. They are hungry for action, and instead of making a million dollars on Wall Street they are making history on the campus.

It should be obvious that you cannot stop the militant students by satisfying their demands. These would-be history makers have stumbled on a terrible secret. They have discovered that the men in power on the campus are too confused, too unsure, too humane, and probably too cowardly to hit back hard. So they are pushing and pushing to see how far they can go.

# Only Stretched Souls Make Music

April 6, 1969

The quality of a social order may be gauged by several criteria: by how effectively it realizes its human resources; by how well it maintains its social plant; and, above, all, by the quality of its people—how self-respecting, benevolent, self-reliant, energetic, etc.

The elimination of profit motive in Communist countries has not made people less greedy and selfish. The increased dependence of the many on the will and whim of the few has not made people more gentle, forbearing and carefree. From all that I read it seems that the attitude of every-man-for-himself is more pronounced in a Communist than in capitalist society.

It was in Communist countries that wives sent their husbands and children, their parents, unhesitatingly, even smugly, to the prisons, the torture room, and the gallows. The compact unity imposed from above has weakened the impulse toward mutual help and voluntary cooperation.

And yet, on the whole, there is less loneliness in a Communist than in capitalist society. People do not feel abandoned and forgotten in a regimented society.

Again and again I come across the assertion that a society cannot grow and thrive without a culturally superior stratum which generates the impulses toward excellence and greatness. The axiomatic assumption is that left to themselves the common people will wallow in sloth or explode in anarchy. The happenings in this country refute this assertion.

In the rest of the world at present there is evidence on every hand that the vigor and health of a society are determined by the quality of the common people rather than that of the cultural elite. It may even be true that the cultural elite performs best when society begins to decay. It was so in Greece, and it seems to be so in contemporary Britain.

Finally, one ought not to equate social health with total harmony, with a lack of contradictions and strains. Actually, vigor and creative flow have their source in internal strains and tensions. It is the pull of opposite poles that stretches souls. And only stretched souls make music.

# In Times of Dangerous Words

**April 13, 1969**

There are times when words and ideas are deemed dangerous, and times when people may profess the most incendiary ideas and proclaim them on housetops without anyone being alarmed.

Obviously, ideas and words are considered dangerous when things are in flux. Thus in the formative days of Christianity, and during the crisis which gave birth to the modern Occident, ideas and words were seen as a sort of explosive. The same is true of our time.

Still it is the presence of a close link between words and deeds which renders the former explosive and dangerous, and such a link is not brought automatically into existence by a fluidity of conditions. In addition to the criticalness of the times there must be also present a relatively large number of "men of words," a certain category of intellectuals, who hover as it were on the borderline between words and action.

This category of intellectuals is made up of people who are basically men of action—potential managers, organizers, administrators—but find themselves encased in the career of "men of words," and see themselves as intellectuals.

They want to act, command, conquer, but being cast in the role of intellectuals they cannot face the reality of their innermost craving. They need the sanction of an absolute truth, a holy cause or an ideal before they can let themselves go. They will grab at any idea or word floating in the air and employ it as an incantation to conjure action out of the void. It is the presence of these action-intellectuals which renders words and ideas dangerous.

The significant point is that since Sputnik the number of action-intellectuals has increased enormously in this country. There has been a fateful change in the tilt of the social landscape. In the past, when the tilt had been toward business, many potential poets and philosophers wound up as businessmen.

But since Sputnik the prestige and material rewards of intellectual pursuits have risen sharply, and many individuals with superb talents for wheeling and dealing are now throwing their weight around on university campuses.

There is of course a good chance that eventually, when they are 40, the present firebrand revolutionaries of the Students for a Democratic Society will be on Wall Street trying to make a million dollars. But right now, at 20, they are explosive and dangerous.

# Israel Stands Alone

April 20, 1969

There is an inevitability—something like a law of nature—about the world's attitude toward Israel. Israel is not allowed to act and react like any other nation. It is expected to be forbearing and long-suffering in the face of provocations no other country would dream of tolerating.

How forbearing and long-suffering would Russia be were it subjected to brigandage, marauding, sabotage, artillery and rocket attacks from several neighboring countries? And how would this country react if armed bands were sent across the border, day in, day out, from Canada and Mexico?

It is good form to be shamelessly brazen when dealing with Israel. A Russia that has despoiled every one of its neighbors says that Israel is expansionist and imperialist, and no one laughs. De Gaulle stops shipments of planes and parts which Israel had bought, and paid for in advance. He also refuses to return the money.

I doubt whether De Gaulle would have dealt thus with the least new nation in darkest Africa. This unheard of brazenness has not diminished the general's popularity with the French people.

Any day now we shall see Americans putting their heads together with French and Russian delegates on how to pressure Israel into doing approximately what the French and the Russians want it to do. Such an agreement at the expense of Israel is supposed to be the beginning of an era of harmony and good will among America, France and Russia.

There is a natural legitimacy about profiting at the expense of Israel.

We are up against a simple, stark fact: The Jews are alone in the world, no commitment by other nations and no alliance can be a factor in the survival of Israel.

America is not defending Israel either diplomatically or militarily. Israel has not received the American planes it wants to buy. No one knows what the Sixth Fleet will do if the Russian navy starts lobbing shells into Israel. The American government is not in the mood to get involved in a new war.

Israel can have no constant friends among the nations. Indeed, Israel's diplomacy must base itself on the assumption that seeming friend are basically neutral or even potential enemies.

For the Jews the Dark Ages are not a thing of the past, buried under strata of centuries, but a virulent plague, momentarily dormant, which may come to life in any country any day.

Israel is the only citadel the Jews have on this planet, and if Israel survives it will be solely because of the dedication and fidelity of Jews everywhere.

# Maintenance: A Trait of the East

## April 27, 1969

The building of the San Francisco Golden Gateway necessitated the mass evacuation of hotels, restaurants, stores and saloons in the neighborhood of the Ferry Building. The buildings stood empty for months waiting for the wrecking crews.

One day I happened to pass by what used to be one of the busiest restaurants on the waterfront and was startled by the sight of two vigorous milkweeds growing against the padlocked doors. The plants grew out of a crack between the sill, worn by innumerable feet, and the tired-looking sidewalk.

The thought which crossed my mind made me laugh: Were the milkweeds casing the joint? Were they the vanguard of nature returning to reclaim and repossess what man has wrought?

★

I may be wrong, but I wonder whether any run-of-the-mill American could see nature repossessing man's work, particularly in a city, without stirrings of misgivings.

Maintenance is one phase of our ceaseless war with nature on this continent. To me there is an aura of grandeur about the dull routine of maintenance: I see it as a defiance of the teeth of time. It is easier to build than to maintain.

Even a lethargic or debilitated population can be galvanized for a while to achieve something impressive, but the energy which goes into maintaining things in good repair day in, day out is the energy of true vigor.

My impression is that the capacity for maintenance is a peculiarity of the Occident and of Japan. Andre Siegfried[95] sees the process of maintenance as something which belongs essentially to the Occidental and thinks it is here that we must look for this distinct characteristic.

It is strange that in Asia, where civilization had its birth, the separation from nature and the ability to hold it at bay should be much less pronounced than in the younger civilization at the Occident. One has the feeling that the true awakening and modernization of a backward country is hardly conceivable without the evolvement of the capacity for maintenance.

There is the story about Georges Clemenceau[96] that when he traveled around the world in 1921 he came to New Delhi and was taken to see the huge office buildings which were just then completed. He stood gazing at the buildings for a long time without uttering a word.

Finally, the British officer who was with him asked what he thought of them. "I was thinking," said Clemenceau, "what ruins, these will make."

As so often with Clemenceau, his chance remark threw a searching light on the human situation. Standing at the heart of Asia, Clemenceau felt himself primarily an Occidental and saw the British Empire as Occidental rather than British.

He also knew that the days of the Occident in Asia were numbered, and that, once the Occident withdrew its hand, the dragon of Asia would move in and sink its yellowed teeth of time into all that the Occident had built and wrought, and gnaw away until naught was left but a skeleton of ruins.

---

[95] André Siegfried (1975-1959), French scholar and writer.
[96] Georges Benjamin Clemenceau (1841-1929), French statesmen and Prime Minister, who influenced the Treaty of Versailles.

# The Weak Help Make Us Human

## May 4, 1969

The formidableness and uniqueness of the human species stem from the survival of the weak. Were it not for the habit of caring for the sick, the crippled and the weak in general humanity could not perhaps have attained culture and civilization. The invalided warrior who had to stay behind while the manhood of the tribe went out to war was probably the first storyteller, teacher and artisan, fashioning weapons and toys.

The earliest development of religion, poetry and wit owed much to the survival of the unfit. One thinks of the unchanged medicine man, the epileptic prophet, the blind bard, the witty hunchback and dwarf. Finally, the sick must have had a hand in the development of the arts of cooking and healing.

The exceptional adaptability of the human species is chiefly a peculiarity of its weak. The difficult and risky task of meeting and mastering the new—whether it be the settlement of new lands or the initiation of new ways or life—is not undertaken by the vanguard of a society but by its rear.

It is the misfits, failures, fugitives, outcasts and their like who are among the first to grapple with the new. Only when, after a clumsy and wasteful struggle, they have somehow bound and tamed the unknown do their betters move in and take charge. The plunge into the new is often an escape from a familiar pattern that is untenable and unpleasant.

It is the weak who strain the ears for a new word, clutch at every promise and rally around a savior and a redeemer. The role the unfit play in human affairs should make us pause whenever we are prompted to see man as a mere animal and not a being of an order apart.

It is probably the weak of the species who took the first steps in the ascent and humanization of man. Chased out of the forest by the strong, they first essayed to walk erect, and in the intensity of their souls first uttered words, and first grabbed a stick to use as weapon and tool.

Man is most peculiarly human when he cannot have his way. His momentous achievements are rarely the result of a clean forward thrust but rather of a soul intensity generated in front of an apparently insurmountable obstacle which bars his way to a cherished goal. It is here that potent words have their birth, and the endless quest, and the stretching of the soul which encompasses heaven and earth.

# The Artist as Eternal Juvenile

**May 11, 1969**

I have been reading Henri Troyat's[97] biography of Tolstoi.[98] There is a sickroom atmosphere about the book. Tolstoi was enormously gifted, enormously perceptive, enormously fortunate, and quite an unpleasant person. Those who knew him well doubted whether he had ever in his life really loved anyone. There is a slimy quality about his ceaseless soul searching, and his self-centeredness bordered on the insane.

It occurred to me as I read that there is not a single great writer or artist I have read about that I would want as a friend, companion or neighbor. Envy, vanity, malice and sheer rudeness seem to be characteristic elements of the creative personality.

There is also this. The sense of uniqueness inherent in the creative process has often inclined the writer and the artist to see themselves at the center of the universe, and as the bearers of a destiny shaped by cosmic forces. Hence their fascination with coincidences, omens and signs. It is a conceit which requires a high capacity for self-dramatization—a capacity indigenous to the juvenile mentality. Other juvenile traits displayed by most writers and artists are an exaggerated reaction, to experience and a compulsion to tell the world about themselves.

★

---

[97] Henri Troyat (1911-2007), Russian/French biographer.
[98] Leo Nikolayevich Tolstoy (1838-1910), Russian realist writer.

Now it may be that the unpleasant qualities of envy, vanity, etc., and the juvenile traits are unavoidable accompaniments of creative striving, and may ease the creative flow. If this is so we ought to be able to put up with them. Yet the mind refuses to accept the inevitability of so aberrant a situation.

There must have been instances where great works were executed by people who felt themselves no more than competent craftsmen. The Paleolithic painters of the breathtaking animal murals in the caves of France and northern Spain, the creators of the fabulous statues of ancient Egypt, the composers of the Old Testament histories, and the craftsmen of the Middle Ages and early Renaissance were without the freakish self-centeredness characteristic of modern writers and artists.

There is apparently an irremediable insecurity at the core of every creative person. Even the most gifted and prolific seem to live the life of eternal, self-doubting. They have to prove their worth each day. They need devotion, recognition, appreciation, prizes and marks of distinction to bolster their confidence: Modern society does not treat its writers and artists as friends and fellow workers, but, at best, as distinguished aliens.

★

All my life I had the feeling that in this country the creative person should not need a sense of uniqueness, a clearly marked separation from the common man, in order to realize and exercise his talents. I snort any time I come across the statement that "all artists want fame, glory, immortality."

It seems to me self-evident that once cultural achievements are considered as worthwhile and useful, and are as munificently rewarded as achievements in business, technology and politics, a mass civilization would be as culturally creative as an aristocratic civilization.

# Fighting Words

**May 18, 1969**

Words are the most unique ingredient of human uniqueness. It has often been said that man is man by virtue of language. What happens to words in a society is, therefore, of vital importance. We have seen in our day now in dehumanized Communist societies the lifeblood is drained out of such potent words as "honor," "truth," "justice," "freedom," "equality," "brotherhood!" Double-talk is one of the earliest symptoms of dehumanization. Stalin's greatest crime was the murder of words.

In this country just, now the debilitation of words is prompted by enraged "men of words" lusting for an apocalyptic denouement. They are yapping in chorus that our affluence is poverty, our freedom slavery, our tolerance oppression, our benevolence greed, and our vigor sickness.

To me it is an alarming symptom that fighting words have lost their bite. We used to have to watch and choose our words not solely for the sake of civilized intercourse but because offensive words spelled trouble. If you insulted a person you often had a fight on your hands.

But right now, student hoodlums, Black Power murder boys and self-styled intellectuals hurl slanderous epithets, screech obscenities and utter threats of murder and arson against teachers, administrators, representatives, officials and police, and nothing happens.

It is imperative that we take insults and threats seriously; that we react swiftly and tellingly against those who say that they will do all they can to create chaos.

# Fashionable Guilt

May 25, 1969

It is probably true that 60% of the adult white population in this country (60% of the white voters) are without a sense of guilt toward the Negro, the poor, and the disadvantaged here and elsewhere. They are ready to help their neighbors and anyone in trouble, but the impulse to help others does not stem from a feeling of guilt.

Most of the 60% started to work for a living in their teens. They had no advantage of wealth or class to give them a jump ahead of their fellow men. Whatever ease, comfort, and security they may enjoy at this moment was achieved by striving and saving through the years. Their white skin did not make life easy for them—did not bring them advantages and privileges. They never felt that the world owed them anything or that they owe anybody—white, black, or yellow—a damn thing.

It is safe to say that most of the people who at present speak and write about this country's difficulties, and have a hand in shaping its policies, do not belong to the 60%. It is the fashion now among educated people to feel uneasy about success—not uneasy enough to give up the fruits of success, but enough to feel guilty about it, and emote soulfully about the grievances of the "disadvantaged," and the defects and sins of the status quo. Right now it is a mark of distinction to have a sense of guilt, and fashionable to confess our sins.

At the 1968 annual convention of the American Bar Association in Philadelphia, speaker after speaker maintained that crime is caused by poverty, ignorance, and, despair, that law and order cannot be maintained until social ills are first cured. The whole tenor of the convention was that we must learn to live with disorder and crime until all ills have been cured and our faulty institutions reformed.

The only defender of law enforcement at this convention of American lawyers was an Englishman, John Passmore Widgery[99], Lord Justice of the Court of Appeals in England. He pointed out that you cannot establish an orderly society solely by curing social ills and by reforming institutions.

The greatest part of England's slums, he said, were razed by the bombings of the last war, and the reforms of the welfare state have practically eliminated poverty. But there has been a steady increase in crime. The reason is that societies throughout the Western world have lost discipline.

---

[99] John Passmore Widgery (1911-1981), Lord Chief Justice of England and Wales, who presided over the now discredited "Bloody Sunday" tribunal.

# The Young Revolution

June 1, 1969

We judge the many by the few. It can't be helped. There are a hundred million youths under 20 in this country, and I cannot help judging them by what several hundreds of them are doing and saying in Berkeley, Chicago and New York.

The young ones are fighting and dying in Vietnam. They are doing the world's work on construction jobs, on docks, on farms, in factories, warehouses, offices and wherever. They are studying in thousands of schools. Many of them are already married and have children. Yet when I think of them it is as if they belonged to a different species.

Sometimes, when I step out of my room, I feel like an immigrant who has just arrived in a strange country. It is hard to immigrate at 66. I do not like what I see. I remember that at the age of 18 I had landed on Skid Row, and spent a third of my life one step ahead of hunger. I cannot help viewing the young of an affluent society as spoiled brats. Now and then I see the irony of the situation: A crabbed old man facing crabbed youth.

Someone tells me that the young have a special talent for diagnosing the evils of our age. I doubt whether it is so. The young have always been dissatisfied. No country is a good country for its young. We are always ill at ease when we have to adjust ourselves and fit in.

The impulse is to change the world to fit us rather than the other way around. The juveniles are natural reformers. But there is no reason why their opinions and judgments should be endowed with a special validity. Actually, in human affairs, wise decisions are more a function of emotional stability than of intellectual brilliance.

Right now the revolution of the young is a revolution against effort, against growth, and above all against apprenticeship. They want instant manhood and power. You sense that the alienation they cry about has its roots in the frustration of the hunger for power. There is no alienation that a little power will not cure.

Growth is unavoidably slow, and all viable achievements are products of growth. The impatient who demand instant results will not achieve anything durable.

Here in San Francisco as I watch the young with their bedrolls hitching rides, and see them sprawled on the grimy sidewalks of Market Street and Haight Ashbury[100], I am reminded strongly of the Great Depression. That the great affluence of the 1960s should produce a phenomenon so similar to that produced by the Great Depression, only substituting children for grownups, is one more striking absurdity of our absurd age.

---

[100] Haight-Ashbury, during 1967, became the epicenter for the "Summer of Love," symbolic of the ensuing "hippie" culture.

# Violent Minority Preys on the Meek

## June 8, 1969

It is a paradox that the most fateful characteristic of our violent age is the non-violence, the incredible submissiveness, of the victims. Hitler and Stalin liquidated millions of men, women and children without meeting serious resistance,

In this country at present, millions of peaceful folk in city streets and ghettos, in suburbs and on campuses are submitting meekly to robbers and muggers, to black and white ideological thugs, and to foul-mouthed insults and threats. No one hits back, and hardly anyone speaks out loud in outrage.

Well-meaning people are warning us not to overreact against those who have turned our cities and schools into savage jungles. We are warned that action by the majority would be vigilantism, that it is the duty of the police to endure taunts and provocations without hitting back, and that we shall not have peace until we have cleansed our souls of racial arrogance and callous smugness.

The other day, at Berkeley, a class of 250 students was addressed by an intruding Negro student as mother... and warned not to come to class the next day or have their throats slit. The punk was not thrown out. The professor, a famous teacher, begged the intruder to leave the class.

Would it have been overreaction or vigilantism had the class rushed the foul-mouthed, bushy faced punk and thrown him out? Was it sheer humaneness that kept the famous professor meek in the face of insults and threats?

The students and professor were plainly afraid. They would probably maintain that they practiced forbearance. When cowardice becomes a fashion its adherents are without number, and it masquerades as forbearance, reasonableness, conscience, and whatnot.

It is amazing how nobly philosophical we became when we have to rationalize our cowardice. We love our enemies, extol altruism, and see self-assertion as the root of evil.

The unavoidable impression is that it is the meekness of the majority that incites and fuels the violence around us. The muggers in the streets, the rioters and looter in the ghettos, the black and white hoodlums on the campuses are all on the lookout for tame enemies and tame battlegrounds.

We do not know what's ahead for us. It is hardly likely that the violent minorities will abruptly change their way. There is a vague feeling that a day of wrath is waiting around the corner, when the saturated resentment of the longsuffering majority crystallizes in retaliation. It is impossible to say where and how the reaction will start.

# The Vulnerable Social Body

### June 15, 1969

It used to be that when you thought of a danger threatening a country's stability and very existence you had an external enemy in mind. Countries were largely afraid of attack or subversion from without. Right now you can count on the fingers of one hand the countries threatened by external enemies.

In most of the world it is domestic strife that threatens social dissolution. In this country it is self-evident that nothing that might possibly happen in Southeast Asia, Europe or the Middle East would have as fateful effects as what is happening in our ghettos and on the campuses.

We have suddenly discovered that the supposedly immortal social body is a vulnerable, fragile thing. A scratch on the social body easily becomes a festering gore. We do not seem to know the first thing about the maintenance of social health and out self-appointed social doctors are the last people to instruct and guide us.

The sociologists tell us that we have to reorder our society, change our attitudes and ways of doing things, and reshape our institutions. Hardly anyone mentions the fact that never before has this country attempted so many drastic reforms and that the result has been strife and turmoil on an unprecedented scale.

Not one sociologist warned us that righting wrongs is a perilous undertaking, that it is hardly likely to prevent violence, and that unless a society is strong enough to maintain order it cannot afford to institute drastic reforms.

Judging by what is happening before our eyes the prescriptions of the sociologists are not for the prevention but for the justification and encouragement of violence. It is also worth noting that the departments of sociology have brought forth some of the nastiest hoodlums on America's campuses.

We are warned not to overreact against rioters, muggers, and vandals who are turning our cities and universities into savage jungles. Yet a review of the recent past indicates that our most critical failure has been not to react immediately and forcefully against the breakers of the public peace.

Those who want us to become inured to violence and learn to live with it are advocating the debasement and corruption of our society.

# In Support of Americans

June 22, 1969

I live in a society full of blemishes and deformities. But it is a society that gives every man elbow room to do the things near to his heart. In no other country is it so possible for a man of determination to go ahead, with whatever it is he sets his heart on, without compromising his integrity.

Of course, those who want acclaim and fortune must cater to other people's demands. But for those who want to be left alone to realize their capacities and talents this is an ideal country. It is incredible how easy it is in this country to cut oneself off from, what one disapproves—from all vulgarity, conformity, speciousness, and other corrupting influences and infections.

The professional detractors of America are telling us day in and day out that we have been debased and dehumanized by our system of government and our way of life. We are told that the majority of the people in this country have no will and no judgment of their own; that we are robots manipulated by politicians, manufacturers and the mass media.

Novelists, playwrights, philosophers and critics often depict this country as a land of the living dead. It is a country where sensitive souls are starved and flayed; where nothing nourishes and everything hurts. Nowhere, they say, is there such a boring monotony: monotony of talk, monotony of ideas, and monotony of outlook on the world.

It is hard to believe that these savage denunciations are based on direct experience with persons and places. I spent half of my life a migratory worker in California, living with people from every state, and the other half as a longshoreman in San Francisco. If now, at age 66, I consult all that I have seen and experienced over the years I find that the people I have lived and worked with all my life had three outstanding qualities:

1—They were skilled people. Working with them you knew beyond doubt that they were intelligent and competent; that they could tackle any problem and often solve it in a subtle original way. They had both technical and social skills so that if dumped anywhere on the planet they could build another America.

2—They needed very little supervision and leadership.

3—They were on the whole wonderfully kind.

All my life I have seen America from below, and what I saw seemed good to me.

# What Do the Young Desire?

**June 29, 1969**

The young of today behave as if they were the first young people in history—as if the older generation had come full grown into the world. Harking to my own adolescence I find most of the grievances of the young specious and pretentious.

They resent the existing system because it tells them "what to do and to be; what kind of thoughts they can think." You ask yourself what this system is and how it tells anyone anything? What is it nowadays in this country that prevents a young man from shaping his life, from realizing his capacities and talents?

Earning a decent living has never been as easy as it is now. Since growth is a do-it-yourself job I cannot see how anyone or anything in this country can prevent a young man from learning and growing, from realizing and exercising his talents, if this is what he really wants. You do not even have to go to college, follow curricula, pass examinations, etc., if what you want is to develop whatever intellectual, artistic and manipulative capacities you may have.

★

When observing protesting adolescents it is safe to assume that they are more subtle and less sensitive than they seem. It is imperative to keep in mind that at least 90% of what adolescents say and do is play-acting and self-dramatization. You can no more explain the style of the young by inner necessity than you can explain fashions in clothes, cooking or speech by inner necessity.

The escape of the young is not from authority, regimentation, mechanization and the like, but from the long haul, the strenuous effort, the long apprenticeship, and the slow, painful ordeal of growth. They are looking for a short cut, the instant fulfillment, the unearned power. They want a ball, an endless entertainment, a 24-hour thriller.

How is it going to end?

A large proportion of the brawling young will end up in the ashcan. The rate of failure among them will be astronomical. The brighter the brawler, the more likely is he to waste himself. Unlike the plodder who never had it easy, the bright ones have not discovered that anything worth having requires toil and sweat. My hunch is also that some of the bright ones will, at 40, try to make a fortune on Wall Street or in real estate.

There are several people I know who were firebrand revolutionaries at 20 and who are now earning $50,000 to $100,000 a year. One of them has made a fortune publishing pornography. He is getting rich and is undermining the system at the same time. He still considers himself a radical, and is a big wheel in the Peace and Freedom Party.

# Elitist Contempt for Americans

July 6, 1969

The anti-Americanism of the foreign intellectual stems not from his fear of the debasing effect America might have on literature, art, music, the cinema, etc., but its effect on the masses. We see again and again how the Americanization of a country results in the de-proletarianization of the workingman.

Americanization means the stiffening of the workingman's backbone, and the sharpening of his appetites. He not only begins to believe that he is as good as anyone else, but wants to live and look like anyone else.

The Americanization of a society amounts to giving it a classless aspect, the sapping of its aristocratic traditions, the diffusion of a sameness which has all the earmarks of equality. And it is this that the foreign intellectual fears and resents.

He not only feels the loss of the grandiose background of mute masses ranged in their millions behind him, but he is also deprived of the aristocratic climate which he feels is vital for the realization and exercise of his creative talents. It is to him a drab, uninspiring world where every mother's son thinks himself as good as anyone else, and the capacity for reverence and worship has become atrophied.

★

Scratch any foreign intellectual, even one ho has lived for decades among us, and you find a would-be aristocrat who loathes the sight, the sound, the smell of common folk. Take Professor

164

Marcuse.[101] This self-styled savior of humanity came to this country in 1934, a refugee from Hitler's Germany.

He has lived among us for over 30 years, and now, in his old age, his disenchantment with this country is spilling over, into book after book. When you brush away the Hegelian double-talk and philosophical flap trap, you discover what it is that is ailing him.

In plain English, Professor Marcuse is offended by the degree to which common people in America are allowed to intrude into the sphere of life which ought to be the preserve of chosen spirits: "to break the peace wherever there is still peace and silence, to be ugly and uglify things, to ooze familiarity, to offend against good form."

Nowhere on this continent is there a spot where Marcuse can escape the sight, the sound and the smell of the vulgar, common Americans.

★

Last summer the professor went to Venice. The place was full of Americans and Americanized vulgarians. In an interview with a reporter for *Il Tempo*[102], Marcuse wondered whether Venice could not be reserved for high-class tourism, so that the hoi polloi would not disturb its solemn beauty.

Marcuse was born in Berlin in 1898. He was in his thirties in the days of The Weimar Republic.[103] As one of the far left he probably, fought the democratic republic as a sham and a swindle and worked for its destruction. Hitler did the destroying. It is worth noting that in 1956 Marcuse had no use for the Hungarian revolution.

---

[101] Herbert Marcuse (1898-1979), German-Jewish academic and political theorist; considered the father of "The New Left" or 1960's socialist activists.
[102] *Il Tempo*, Italian daily newspaper headquartered in Rome since 1944.
[103] Weimar Republic, pre-Hitler parliamentary republic of Germany; est. 1919.

# Have the Evils of the Past Left Us?

July 13, 1969

It is a mark of modern man's desperate need for pride that he finds the weight of sin much lighter than the weight of weakness. It is disconcerting that despite its monstrous transgressions under Hitler, Germany seems yet the one European nation with an unimpaired pride,

Defeat in World War II had not blurred the awareness in most minds that no nation by itself—however vast in territory, population, and resources—was Germany's match; that it needed the mobilization of the whole world to bring Germany to its knees. Thus the Germans alone among the Europeans are not oppressed by a vitiating sense of impotence, and it is their unimpaired pride which accounts for their astounding capacity for recovery.

It is doubtful whether there can be such a thing as a collective sense of remorse; collective resentment yes, and, of course, collective pride and elation, but not shame. The association with others is almost always felt as an association with our betters, and to sin with our betters cannot be productive of a crushing feeling of shame. When we are members of a compact group we are perhaps incapable of shame. It is only as individuals distantly associated with a group that the deeds of the group can blemish our self-respect.

Yet if history is not to repeat itself it is imperative that nations keep alive memories of past crimes, mistakes, and failures. Such memories can be a more potent source of social health than memories of past glories. One thinks of France fasting on the anniversary of the surrender to Hitler. So, too, Germany's task of cleansing itself of the taint of the Nazi era might be aided by a yearly day of fasting and prayer. The day should perhaps coincide with the Jewish day of atonement (Yom Kippur) and some of the prayers should be translations from the Hebrew.

As we near the three-quarter mark of the century we seem less certain than ever before that the apocalyptic evils we have witnessed since World War I are behind us. The unanticipated Russian invasion of Czechoslovakia has crystallized the recognition that colonialism has been transferred from the East to the West. The future wars of liberation will be fought in Europe. The resurgence of anti-Semitism in Russia revives the threat of a final solution.

Is it totally impossible that one morning we shall learn that the Russians have decided to harass their Jews from the earth? Nor can we tell what the rapidly escalating Negro problem in this country is leading to. And what effect would defeat and humiliation in Vietnam have on America?

One has the feeling that the 20th century will be a continuous hell to the end—one crisis after another, until all passions have burned themselves out.

# The Source of Real Pride

July 20, 1969

To an impartial onlooker it seems preposterous that Negroes in America in their hunger for pride should reach out all the way to Africa rather than try to derive it from Negro achievements on this continent.

Twenty-two million black Americans are lots of people, and they live in the midst of one of the most technically advanced societies on this planet. It would be the most natural thing for black Americans to be the vanguard of black people everywhere, to show what Negro enterprise, intelligence and guts can achieve, and to be the big brother to the backward poor countries in Africa.

What we see instead is 22 million black Americas sitting around waiting for their backward, poor African brothers to hurry up and make history so that the well-fed, well-dressed black Americans could have some pride.

Most Negro spokesmen in America are utterly convinced that the only way to have something is to get it from someone else. Do-it-yourself is too slow, too uncertain, and too difficult. They want the pride and the power that come in cans.

The other day Dr. S.D. Onabanjo, a visitor from Nigeria, had this to say to a Harlem audience on the subject of Afro-American studies.

"You are not Africans. We Africans have enough trouble try-ing to help out our own people. If black Americans gave us the money and technical assistance the American Jews provide for Israel there would be no problem. But the few that can don't seem interested. You have wonderful black orators, but we don't need that. We need scientists, teachers, tool-and-die makers, doctors and dentists, bricklayers and skilled carpenters. You black Americans are trying to find a past, and we Africans are trying to find a future."

America is the last stop and the last chance for everybody. If the Negro cannot make it here, he won't make it anywhere.

# Rudeness, the Fanatic's Weapon

## July 27, 1969

Rudeness is the weak man's imitation of strength. Nothing so illustrates the incurable insecurity of the fanatical mentality as the affinity between fanaticism and rudeness. The family likeness between fanatics of diametrically opposed persuasions, such as the Nazis and the Communists, is partly due to the homogenizing effect of rudeness.

It is of course true that rudeness bolsters the fanatic's intolerance. It throttles the soft amenities which would dovetail him with others, and blur his uncompromising stance. Thus it is generally true that eras of blind faith are areas of bad manners. On the other hand, as Francis Bacon observed, "the times inclined to unbelief are civil times."

Right now the paragons of rudeness are found on the campuses and among people who fancy themselves in the vanguard of society. Obscenities have become a mark of sophistication, of idealism, and of attained manhood. Rudeness is now serving as a substitute for power, for faith, and for achievement.

To me, the present escalation of rudeness is an indication that the apocalyptic Stalin-Hitler madhouse is by no means behind us. The yammering, screeching, obscene student hoodlums and Black Power murder boys demand instant power and instant bliss are "final solutionists" of the Stalin-Hitler brand.

Sen. Ribicoff[104] displayed historical illiteracy when he accused Mayor Daley[105] and the Chicago police of being Gestapo.[106] It was precisely because the Weimar Republic had no Daleys and no Chicago police to fight its battles in Germany's cities during the 1920s that the Nazis and their Gestapo came to power. It is never the police who start a police state. The opposite has been true; the "final solutionists" serve their apprenticeship fighting the police.

There is no getting away from it: If the mass of people in this country are not ready to strengthen the hand of their police or find some way of reacting quickly and forcefully against those who are determined to disrupt and destroy our institutions, we shall be heading toward a Fascist state and eventual holocaust.

The middle has up to now remained silent and inert. One is conscious of a dark resentment welling up in the majority. But, so far, no one has tried to channel the pent-up resentment into active resistance. It might perhaps be better for this country if the middle were to burst out in anger now and then, than that it brood impotently, and wait and pray for a Hitler.

---

[104] Abraham A. Ribicoff (1910-1998), U.S. Senator; also served the President John F. Kennedy administration as Health Secretary.

[105] Richard J. Daley (1902-1976), Chicago Mayor (1955-1976); served during the 1968 Democratic Presidential Convention riots and the "Chicago Seven" trial.

[106] Gestapo, Nazi secret state police.

# The Limit of Sociologists

August 3, 1969

Is there any proof that sociologists can impartially diagnose a social ailment and prescribe an effective remedy?

It is preposterous that the same sociologists who fostered some of the most violent hoodlums on our campuses should be accepted as impartial scientists and be paid large sums to prescribe cures for violence. Much of the sociological writing on the nature of poverty and violence is sheer hogwash.

For some obscure reasons, most sociologists have a mordant contempt for the status quo, and are particularly hostile towards Congress and the police. Why this hostility should be characteristic of sociologists and not of political scientists is a mystery. And why do they single out Congress and the police? Perhaps because these two bodies are most representative of common people.

The self-appointed doctors of our social body are profoundly convinced of the dullness, narrowness, selfishness, vulgarity and dishonesty of the common man. And nothing so demonstrates to the sociologist the degeneracy of the common man as his championing of the police.

The poverty program initiated and run by sociologists aimed not to help the poor but to radicalize and rouse them. There was a deliberate attempt to use the poor to bring down "the whole rotten structure."

One cannot resist the impression that many sociologists have a vested interest in turmoil and violence and do all they can to advance that interest. They reject the demand for law and order on the grounds that those who raised it were not intelligent enough to comprehend fully any complex issue or else had something other in mind than the concern for public safety.

The sociologists are advocating drastic reforms as a cure for all of our ills. They do not seem to know, and certainly never mention, that drastic reform is a perilous undertaking, that a society must gird its loins and expect the worst when it sets out to purge itself overnight of every unjust practice and objectionable habit.

Whereas medical doctors when they prescribe a new drug warn the patient against dangerous side-effects, our social doctors assume that their prescribed reforms can never go wrong.

You hardly ever come across a sociologist involved in some social project who insists on the limits of his knowledge and methodology.

# Human Nature Offers No Guarantees

## August 10, 1969

We do not love humanity when we expect too much from people. Imperfection is one of the central attributes of man's uniqueness. There is a perfect ant, a perfect bee, etc., but man is incurably unfinished and imperfect. Not only is man an unfinished, defective animal, lacking specialized organs and organic adaptations, but he is also an unfinished man. Man's goal in life is still to become and stay human.

Man became human by breaking away from nature, by getting out from under the iron necessities which dominate and imprison other forms of life. But the separation from nature is never complete. There is still an enclave of nonhuman nature locked in the dark cellars of our mind.

No matter how effectively man dominates the nature that is around him, he can never succeed in completely taming the nature, the beast, that is within him. We are still to some extent devils— beasts masquerading as men.

The inescapable predicament of the human condition is that the good and the evil in us are so intertwined that they cannot be kept apart. We have seen it happen before our eyes. The ills and woes which at present convulse our society and strain it to the breaking point were born of a concerted effort to right wrongs; to give equality to the Negro, improve the lot of the poor, and throw open the gates to education and self-advancement. No one cautioned us that the onrush of reforms may turn our society into an apocalyptic madhouse.

The 20th century, which has seen unimaginable slaughter and destruction, has also seen unprecedented attempts to realize dreams, visions, and wild hopes. Some of the worst tyrannies of our time were instituted by men genuinely dedicated to the welfare of humanity.

As we near the three-quarter mark of the century, it ought to be self-evident that when a society sets out to purge itself of inequities and shortcomings it should expect the worst, and ready itself for a crisis that would test its stability and stamina. Only a vigorous, orderly society can aspire to become a wholly just society overnight.

In human affairs there is no certainty that good follows from good, and evil from evil. There is always the danger that the attempt to eliminate evil would be like an ill purging which takes away the good with the bad.

# A Joyless Youth

What strikes me about today's young is their lack of zest. Their obscenities sound mechanical and wooden, and their insolence is without sparkle. They dissipate without pleasure, and are vain without a purpose. Never have the young taken themselves so seriously. The young voices on the steps of Sproul Hall[107] are tired teachers' voices.

You have the impression that the young want to teach before they learn, want to retire before they work, want to rot before they ripen. And they want everything to happen instantly; instant manhood, instant diplomas, instant power and instant bliss. They cannot bide their time because it is not the time of their growth.

The activists on the campus are telling university administrators and the faculty what's wrong with the curriculum, the teaching and the university's attitude toward the world. In between lecturing the faculty, the deans and the chancellors tell the country what's wrong with its way of life, its power structure and whatnot. They know everything without thinking, without learning and without experiencing. And there is no one to tell them to shut their mouths and to slap them down.

The confrontation seen on campuses everywhere is between clumsy insolence and cowardice masquerading as reasonableness.

---

[107] Sproul Hall, UCLA, Berkeley; named for former university president Robert Gordon Sproul; site of student protests during the 1960s.

No one seems to have discovered the simple fact that with activists a soft answer does not turn away but invites wrath.

It is of interest that when in 1964 white student activists went to Mississippi to give a hand with voter registration they displayed the same arrogance and ignorance we are now witnessing on the campuses. The moment they arrived they behaved like experts and authorities on all matters concerning the Negro and civil rights. They did all the talking with very little listening.

Eventually they were slapped down and kicked out by the Negro workers who sensed that the white students were using the black community as a stage for their anti-social acting out, that they joined the civil rights movement for their own personal needs and hangups.

The hope is often expressed that student activism eventually may lead to genuine educational reform, provided an exasperated public does not lose patience and overreact. Is such a hope justified?

★

I remember how four years ago when Savio[108] and his Free Speech movement colleagues started their revolution on the Berkeley campus I had the feeling that I was witnessing the Latin-Americanization of an American university. The politicization of universities has been for decades a fact of life below the Rio Grande.

But I have still to hear anyone maintain that education and academic performance in Latin America have attained some sort of excellence not found in institutions of learning untouched by a student revolution.

---

[108] Mario Savio (1942-1996), American political activist and key member of Berkeley's Free Speech Movement.

# God and the Machine Age

### August 24, 1969

It sounds odd in modern ears that Jehovah played a vital role in the rise of the scientific and technological civilization of the modern Occident. It is hard for us to realize how God-conscious were the men active at the birth of modern science. Jehovah was to them the supreme mathematician and technician who had created the world and set it going.

To unravel the mysteries of nature was to decipher God's text and rethink his thought. So convinced was Johann Kepler[109] that in discovering the laws of planetary motion he was deciphering God's book of the world, he boasted in exaltation that God the author had to wait 6,000 years for His first reader.

Leonardo da Vinci[110] paused in his dissection of corpses to pen a prayer: "Would that it might please the Creator that I were able to reveal the nature of man and his customs even as I describe his figure." To da Vinci, living creatures were wondrous machines devised by a master mechanic, and he wanted to take them apart and discover how they were built and how they worked.

By observing and tinkering with God's machines, man could himself become a maker of machines. One could perhaps even-

---

[109] Johann Kepler (1571-1630), German mathematician, astronomer, and astrologer, who established the laws of planetary motion.
[110] Leonardo da Vinci (1452-1519), Italian polymath with expertise spanning from art to science.

tually build a seeing mechanism, a hearing mechanism, a flying machine, and so on. The making of machines would be a second creation: man's way of breathing will and thought into matter.

It is conceivable that modern science and technology might have developed as they did without a particular conception of God. Yet it almost seems that the Occident had first to have a God who was a scientist and an engineer before it could create a civilization dominated by science and technology.

For all we know, one of the reasons that other civilizations, with all their ingenuity and skills, did not develop a machine age, is that they lacked a God whom they could readily turn into an all-powerful engineer. For has not the mighty Jehovah performed from the beginning of time the feats that our machine age is even now aspiring to achieve?

He shut up the sea with doors and said: "Hitherto shalt thou come but no further; and here shall thy proud waves be stayed." He made pools of water in the wilderness and turned the desert into a garden. He numbered the stars and called them by name. He commanded the clouds, and told rivers whither to flow. He measured the waters in the hollow of His hand, and metered out the heaven with the span, and comprehended the dust in a measure and weighed the mountains in scales.

# The Difficulty of Change

**August 31, 1969**

To know the central problems of an age is to have our fingers on a thread of continuity through the welter of willful events and unforeseen crises.

It is my contention that the main challenge of our age is drastic change—from backwardness to modernity, from subjection to equality, from poverty to affluence, from work to leisure. These are all highly desirable changes, changes that mankind has hoped and prayed for through the millennia. Yet it is becoming evident that, no matter how desirable, drastic change is the most difficult and dangerous experience mankind has undergone.

We are discovering that broken habits can be more painful and crippling than broken bones, and that disintegrating values may have as deadly a fallout as disintegrating atoms.

In this country change seems familiar and acceptable. We seem to change homes, jobs, habits, friends, even husbands and wives, without much difficulty.

Yet a moment's reflection will show that change such as the world has seen during the past 150 years is something wholly unprecedented and unique in mankind's experience. From the beginning of recorded history down to the end of the 18th century the way of life of the average man living in the civilized centers of the earth had remained substantially the same.

To the Arab historian Ibn Khaldoon[111] it was self-evident that "past and future are as alike as two drops of water." Even in this

---

[111] Ibn Khaldūn (1332-1406), Northern African historiographer, forerunner to modern historian.

country people lived in 1800 A.D. the way they lived in 3000 B.C. A greater gulf lies between us and Washington[112] than lay between him and the Egyptian farmers who labored for Cheops.[113]

The end of the 18th century marks a sharp dividing line between an immemorial static world and a world of ceaseless change. It is obvious, therefore, that change is far from being as natural and matter-of-fact as we imagine it to be. Moreover, an observant person will notice that even in this country change is never free of irritation and elements of fear.

And, if we had to change our whole way of life as the backward and disadvantaged have to do when they are determined to catch up with the rest of the world overnight, we too would become upset and unbalanced.

---

[112] George Washington (1732-1799), 1st U.S. President; military and political leader during the American Revolution.

[113] Khufu or "Cheops," Pharaoh of Ancient Egypt from approx. 2589-2566 B.C.; builder of the Great Pyramids of Giza.

# The God of Humankind

September 7, 1969

In exploring the differences between civilizations, their attitude toward nature should be given a prominent place. This attitude not only affects religion but determines the pattern of freedom and power, and the position of the individual. It is doubtful whether a population awed by nature can savor freedom or know how to resist arbitrary power.

The downgrading of nature in the Old Testament—God created both nature and man but made man in his own image, and enjoined him to subdue the earth—has been at the root of the Occident's aspiration toward freedom and justice, and of its science and technology which enabled it to master nature on an unprecedented scale. The ancient Hebrews were the first to enunciate a clear-cut separation between man and nature, and their role in the humanization of man cannot be overstated.

God is that which makes man human, and the devil is that which dehumanizes him. The only valid theology is the theology of man's soul. It is in the soul, not in Heaven, that God and the devil are in perpetual combat; and it is this theology of the soul which constitutes the meaning of history. For history has meaning only when it is a history of humanization. If either God or the devil wins a total victory history will come to an end.

Man is utterly fantastic when seen as an animal, a God, a machine or a physiochemical complex. Nothing makes man so fantastically unfamiliar as when he is likened to something familiar. To forget that man is a fantastic creature is to ignore his most crucial trait.

Think of man's most fantastic invention—God. Man invents God in the image of his longings, in the image of what he wants to be, then proceeds to imitate that image, vie with it, and strive to overcome it. He prays to and abases himself before his God, revolts against Him, and in the process generates undreamed-of energies. Man's fiction becomes a vital part of his environment, and he is shaped by it. If this is not fantastic, what is?

To feel wholly at home in the world is to partake of the nature of plants and animals. Man is an eternal stranger in this world. He became a stranger when he cut himself off from the rest of creation and became human. From this incurable strangeness stem our incurable insecurity, our unfulfillable craving for roots, our passion to cover the world with manmade compounds, our need for a God who appoints us His viceroy on earth.

# A Longing for Power

September 14, 1969

Who has power in America?

On the San Francisco waterfront, the shipowners can neither hire nor fire me, nor can they direct me how to do my job. All they can do is to tell me what they want done, and I am supposed to surprise them by my ingenuity.

In the colleges and high schools of the Bay Area, presidents, chancellors, deans, principals and teachers are being insulted and terrorized by white and black student hoodlums. No one has the power to slap down the brazen adolescents and chase them off the campuses.

Again in the Bay Area, the police are spat upon, called pigs, and now and then gunned down by Black Panther murder boys.

Finally, we have seen a President of the United States and his secretary of state afraid to show their faces in New York lest they be reviled by a pack of idealistic hoodlums.

Everywhere you look in America, the so-called power structure seems powerless. The confrontation is between insolence and almost paralyzed authority.

It should be evident, therefore, that people who lust for power are not likely to be happy in America. Here, neither money nor education nor office nor connections enable a person to attain power. The opportunities in America are for learning, experience, money, achievement, comfort, freedom, but not for power.

Seen against this background, the brazen clamor for black power and student power seems ridiculous. One suspects that this naive reaching out for power masks an escape from the burdens and trials of freedom. A generation that revolts against striving, patient preparation, and strenuous learning equates freedom with effortlessness and power with instant satisfaction.

It could be, of course, that the clamor for power is a clamor for manhood. The black power boys and the student activists are proving their manhood by calling everyone in sight a mother… and by creating disorder in streets, on campuses, in political conventions, etc.

And yet in the case of the Negro it might be true that he needs a taste of power to cure his soul. But the Negro's only way to power is through organization. Organization is an accumulation of power without the possession of instruments of coercion; but organization requires trust. So long as there is no mutual trust among Negroes there will be no black power.

# Our Future Might Be in the Past

**September 21, 1969**

The other day the thought occurred to me that our era of rapid, drastic, ceaseless change is perhaps an interlude that is nearing its end. After all, change such as the world has been experiencing for a century or so is unprecedented in man's stay on this planet, and utterly foreign to any other form of life.

It is indeed questionable whether life can endure and thrive in an environment so lacking in continuity. It is plausible, therefore, that what is waiting for us around the corner is not an utterly novel future but an immemorial past.

Are there portents of such a return to be seen in our midst?

There is no doubt that the totalitarian societies of our time, whether of the right or of the left, are a return to the past, the ancient past of the river-valley civilizations, where everything was planned, predetermined, and minutely supervised by a huge bureaucracy made up of scribes with their papyrus rolls or clay tablets, and overseers with their whips.

It is of interest that almost a century ago the Swiss historian Jacob Burckhardt[114] foresaw this form of a return to the past. In a letter to a friend he predicted the time when life would become a supervised stint of misery, daily begun and ended to the sound of drums.

The clamor of our scribes (intellectuals) for power should be seen as a reaching out for the distant past... If there is anything certain it is this: Wherever the scribes attain power they create a

---

[114] Jacob Burckhardt (1818-1897), Swiss historian of art and culture.

**186**

social order that is both hierarchical and regimented. No matter how idealistic, an intelligentsia in power becomes a priviligentsia. They'll probably call such a social order a New Democracy, but it will be a Minocracy.

Another symptom of a return to the past is the recent explosive self-assertion of adolescents. All through the past young adults have acted effectively as members of political parties, creators of business enterprises, advocates of new doctrines and leaders of armies.

The middle-aged came into their own with the advent of the middle class during the 19th century. Even now young men of both the aristocracy and the working class are more in touch with the realities of power than the young of the middle class.

Thus the present revolt of middle class adolescents is an attempt to reestablish a social pattern which had been disrupted by the industrial revolution.

# The Passage to Manhood

**September 28, 1969**

The key to much of the violence in our society seems to lie with the young. Youth accounts for an ever-increasing percentage of crime against property and persons, going well beyond their steadily increasing percentage of the population. About 75% of the persons arrested for robbery are under 25. The thrust of much of the violence in the streets, in the ghettos and on the campuses is provided by young people.

The peak years for crimes of violence are from 18 to 20, followed by the 21 to 24 age group. These are the years of the most drastic change in the life of the individual—the change from boyhood to manhood. It is a paradox of our time that just when we are learning to master drastic changes in every department of life, the familiar, immemorial change from boyhood to manhood has become difficult and explosive.

We have no puberty rites which would routinize and ease the boy's passage to manhood. In the past boys used to prove their manhood by going to work—by doing a man's work and getting a man's pay. But right now large numbers of juveniles, both in the poor and the well-off segments of the population, are kept, by unemployment or prolonged schooling, from having a share in the world's work. They remain suspended between boyhood and manhood, lacking the sense of usefulness and worth which comes from a useful, well-paying job. Crime in the streets and obscene insolence on the campuses are in some degree sick forms of self-assertion and of proving one's manhood.

It should be obvious that we cannot begin to cure the sickness of our time unless we devise means for smoothing the passage from boyhood to manhood. It is imperative that every boy and girl on reaching the age of 17 should be given an opportunity, or even be compelled, to spend three years earning a living at top wages. They should have a right to a job. There is an enormous backlog of work to be done both inside and outside the cities. Federal, state and city governments, and also business and labor, will have to pool their resources to supply the jobs and the necessary training.

The routinization of the passage from boyhood to manhood will contribute to the solution of many of our pressing problems. I cannot think of any other undertaking that will dovetail so many of our difficulties into an opportunity for healthy, orderly growth.

An Afterthought: I remember reading somewhere that in South Africa among certain tribes work in the mines has replaced the ritual related to puberty. It used to be that a young man had to kill a lion or an enemy tribesman to prove he was a man. Today, many young natives do not feel they have arrived until they put in a stint in the mine.

# Common People Make History

**October 5, 1969**

It still is an article of faith of historians that common people, the masses, do not make history. Here is a recent statement: "The masses are the historical empty space in which events occur." The rising importance of the masses in modern times has filled the minds of historians with foreboding. Even so humane an historian as Karl Jaspers[115] sees the masses as a dead weight, "an immense gravitational pull which paralyzes every upward sweep." According to Freud, "The masses are lazy, unintelligent, always ready to give free rein to their indiscipline."

History, we are told, is made by elites, by minorities, and the masses move and act only when stirred by the ideas and impulses generated by the elites.

One wonders, therefore, whether the historians are watching the contemporary scene, and whether they are aware of the peculiar role the masses play at present in shaping the fate of nations.

Take Britain for instance: British scientists, technologists, thinkers, writers, artists and administrators are performing as brilliantly as ever before. The British elites are as good as any, yet Britain is ailing and in a state of decline. The British economy is tottering from one crisis to another, and the reason is that the masses refuse to perform.

To produce the same piece of machinery, Britain needs twice as many men as Sweden, and four times as many as the United

---

[115] Karl Jaspers (1883-1969), German psychologist and philosopher who emphasized humanism.

States. Nothing the brilliant British economists, planners, and managers can think up has any effect.

The readiness to work has become the great mystery of our time. Everywhere we look we can see how the health and vigor of a society are determined not by the quality of the elites, but by the temper and the habits of the common people.

It is a mistake to believe that the dynamism of a population depends on the quality of the leaders. The truth is just the opposite —the effectiveness of the leaders depends upon the capacities for effort and enterprise which the people possess.

In the free world at present the elites of various countries have enough characteristics in common to form a group. You can visualize them assembled in one enclave, living together, not necessarily in harmony, but with no insurmountable barriers in ways of though and of action. The striking differences we can see between economies, nations, and civilizations derive mainly from the makeup of the masses.

# The Arrogant Minority

**October 12, 1969**

Most often in history the oppressed were a vast majority facing a privileged minority entrenched in the status quo. In America, at present, those who feel underprivileged constitute a minority, and the status quo is defended by a vast majority.

It is of course true that ours is an age of minorities. Everywhere we look we see minorities throwing their weight around and boxing the ears of the majority. Still it is doubtful whether even the wildest black power enthusiast entertains the possibility of an incohesive, undisciplined, and unskilled Negro minority imposing itself on the white majority.

If it be true, as the black power militants say, that there is a colonial situation in America, then it is a strange sort of colonialism where the colonialists are not only nine times the number of the "colonialees," but also do most of the hard work.

We hear it endlessly repeated that South Africa is on the brink of catastrophe because it tries to hold down 15 million Negroes with only 3½ million whites. The same people also tell us that we are on the brink of chaos because 180 million white Americans are not doing the right thing fast enough for 22 million Negroes. And we are given to understand that this country, with an overwhelming white majority, and with an unprecedented effort to right the Negroes' wrongs, is nearer a breakdown than South Africa.

The advocacy of nonresistance in the face the black power threat will not promote racial reconciliation and harmony but is more likely to destroy race relations, and delay Negro progress for decades.

Idealistic hoodlums are hoodlums first and should be treated as such. Ideals are a dime a dozen, and much of the time they are fig leaves to cover a lust for power and self-aggrandizement.

Right now in the Bay Area, some 500 Negro students, backed by some leaders of the Negro community, are issuing shrill, dictatorial edicts and demand the unconditional surrender of San Francisco State College which has over 17,000 white students. It is one more example of ingrained Negro opinion that if you want something you do not work for it but demand that others give it to you. All you have to do is be brazen enough and push hard enough.

# The Unmined Talent of the Masses

## October 19, 1969

The accepted view is that talent and genius are rare exceptions —happy flukes of nature. Anyone who maintains that talent and genius are common, that the mass of people are lumpy with unrealized potentialities, usually meets unbelief or derision. The majority of scholars and writers hug the opinion that the anonymous populace is a waste product and a dead weight.

Yet there is evidence that the masses are a mine rich with all conceivable capacities. The trouble is that there is no science or expertise of talent-mining. We have to wait for chance and circumstance to wash nuggets out of the hidden veins, and bring them to the surface.

We know of a few instances where the masses were shaken up, churned, shoveled and scattered so that their talent-content became visible. The dumping of millions of common people from Europe on this continent was such a churning and scattering.

A more sanguinary experiment on the masses was performed by Stalin in Russia. Stalin liquidated the most intelligent, cultivated, and gifted segment of the Russian population and then proceeded to extract every conceivable talent and aptitude from the tortured Russian masses. It was a cruel, wasteful way, yet no one will maintain that the Russian people are at present less endowed with talent than they were before the Bolshevik[116] revolution.

---

[116] Bolsheviks were the precursor to the Communist Party of the Soviet Union.

During the Renaissance, there were several instances of an almost sudden activation of the creative power of the masses. We are told that Florence at the time of the Renaissance had more artists than citizens. Where did the artists come from? They were for the most part the sons of shopkeepers, artisans, peasants, and petty officials.

Giotto[117] and Andrea del Castagno[118] were sheepherding boys. Ghirlandajo[119] was the son of a goldsmith. Andrea del Sarto[120] the son of a tailor. Donatello[121] the son of a wool carder. Most of the artists served their apprenticeship with artisans and craftsmen. The art honored in Florence was a trade, and the artists were treated as artisans.

Art was in the air. Everyone in Florence seemed to know something about the procedures and techniques of the arts, and could judge whatever work was in progress. There was also a sort of spotting system. There were discerning eyes watching the young for marks of talent.

When a sheepherding boy picked up a piece of charcoal from the pavement and started to draw on the wall there was someone who saw it and asked the boy whether he would like to draw and paint, an in this way Andrea del Castagno became a painter.

Something similar happened in Holland during its "Golden Century"—roughly 1600-1700 A.D. A nation of about a million inhabitants produced several thousand painters, among them Hals[122], Rembrandt, and Vermeer.[123] After 1700, Dutch painting sharply declined and has never recovered.

---

[117] Giotto di Bondone (1266-1337), Italian painter and architect.
[118] Andrea del Castagno (1421-1457), Italian Renaissance painter.
[119] Ghirlandajo (1400s), name given to a family of Italian Renaissance artists.
[120] Andrea del Sarto (1486-1531), Italian Renaissance painter.
[121] Donatello di Niccolò di Betto Bardi (1386-1466), Italian artist and sculptor.
[122] Fran Hals (1580-1666) & Dirck Hals (1591-1656), Dutch painters; brothers.
[123] Johannes Vermeer (1632-1675), Dutch painter.

# Nature is Mankind's Real Enemy

### October 26, 1969

My unworshipful attitude toward nature is continuously getting me into trouble. My contention that the harmony between man and nature must be a harmony designed and dictated by man is angrily rejected by all sorts of people, but most vehemently by the educated. It is a mark of intellectual distinction nowadays to run down men and extol nature.

The attitude of the educated toward nature is particularly grotesque when you hear a Latin American or an American intellectual enthuse about nature. About two years ago, I had a visitor from Peru. He said that he was a professor of sociology and also a novelist and a poet. He had with him a Peruvian student from Berkeley to do the translating. He was traveling in this country as a guest of the State Department. I let him talk.

He said that if it was unfortunate that this country was so far ahead; how the attempt to catch up with us distorts and cripples other countries. I asked how he liked San Francisco. "Not bad," he said, but he was disgusted with the Golden Gate Park. How dared we play such tricks on nature! The artificial mountains, lakes, creeks, and waterfalls were a blasphemy—we made nature jump at our bidding.

I said: "You come from a country where nature has repossessed all that the Incas had built, through centuries, with infinite toil. All the wonderful terraces, canals, roads, bridges and cities have become wilderness. Nature is snatching the bread from your mouth. Your one and only problem is how to cope with nature, and your wildest dreams should be a Peru turned into a Golden Gate Park. Yet you go on mouthing the inane clichés about nature that you have picked up on the left bank in Paris from posturing two-bit intellectuals.

He stood up, a picture of outraged dignity. The Peruvian student from Berkeley had a twinkle in his eyes—we exchanged winks. About a year later I read that President Fernando Belaúnde Terry[124] of Peru, on opening a network of rural dirt roads, said, "In Peru nature is our enemy!" I wondered whether my professor was present and walked out on his president.

As to Africa: We tend to forget that in Africa the battle that has to be won is not against colonialism but against nature. The chatter of the African leaders about sovereignty, Negritude and African destiny is totally irrelevant to the central task which is the conquest of African nature, primeval, relentless, aggressive, that has enslaved and degraded man to an extent unknown anywhere else.

The enemies in Africa are the forests, the rivers, the deserts, disease, and brutalization. Man may have originated in Africa, but he had to move away from the cruel anti-human, continent to unfold his unique capacities.

---

[124] Fernando Belaúnde Terry (1912-2002), elected Peruvian president in 1963-1968 and in 1980-1985, bookending eleven years of military rule.

# Intellectuals in Exile

November 2, 1969

No one has recorded what Herbert Marcuse said when he came to this country in 1934 from Hitler's Germany. It is safe to assume that he did not immediately see Americans as one-dimensional men, and did not equate their tolerance with oppression, their freedom with slavery, and their good nature with simplemindedness.

We have a record of what several other German-speaking intellectuals said when they arrived in the 1930s. It is worth quoting in full the words of Olga Schnitzler, the widow of the Viennese novelist, Arthur Schnitzler[125]:

"So much is here to learn and to see. Everyone has been given an opportunity. Everyone who has not been completely worn out experiences here a kind of rebirth. Everyone feels what a grandiose, complex and broad-minded country America is, how well and free one can live among those people without perfidy and malice. Yes, we have lost a homeland, but we have found a world."

Once they became American citizens and acquired a fat bank account, many of these intellectuals began to feel constrained and stifled by the forwardness and the mores of the plebian masses. They missed the aristocratic climate of the Old World.

Inevitably, too, they became disdainful of our lowbrow, practical intelligence. They began to doubt whether Americans had the high-caliber intelligence to formulate an adequate foreign policy or solve the pressing problems of an atomic age.

---

[125] Arthur Schnitzler (1862-1931), Austrian writer, often controversial.

Hardly one of them bethinks himself that in Europe where intellectuals of their kind have all along had a hand in managing affairs, things have not gone too well. Something in them prevents them from sensing the unprecedented nature of the American experiment; that the rejected of Europe have come here together, tamed a savage continent in an incredibly short time, and fashioned the finest society on a large scale the world has so far seen.

# The Cost of Revolution

**November 9, 1969**

To some people "revolution" is a holy word. Anyone who is against revolution is a hater of humanity. The fact that revolutions which occurred in our time are national-socialist, lead to social fascism, and that Stalin, Mao, Ho Chi Minh and Castro have more in common with Hitler than with capitalists of any sort, does not register in their minds. They deny that Hitler had a revolution. If you mention that Lenin and Stalin between them caused the death of some 50 million men, women, and children, they foam at the mouth.

These worshippers of revolution are mostly middle-aged radicals. Back in their youth they dreamed of revolution, and now on the threshold of old age they try to recapture their youth by a show of adulation for the black and white young revolutionaries. Any time they hear of violence in the ghettoes or on the campuses they get a thrill. Quite a number of them savor the exquisite luxury of feeling alienated on $50,000 a year.

It staggers the mind that grownup persons who have witnessed the horror and slaughter, the incredible suffering and degradation brought about by the Russian and German revolutions should still hope and pray for a revolution.

The revolution started by Lenin had the earmarks of a natural calamity. Its consequences were more gruesome than those of the most virulent form of pestilence. If, in 1917, the German government, instead of moving Lenin and his fellow conspirators in a sealed car toward the Russian frontier, had smuggled a car loaded with the cultures of the most deadly plague microbes, the results would have been less freighted with frightfulness and death.

It is estimated that the "Black Death" which visited Europe in the 14th century, and which is considered one of the worst disasters in the history of the Occident, killed 25 million people. And although the Black Death microbe seemed to have had an affinity for clergy and university students, it did not extirpate the most enterprising and talented segment of the population as did the Lenin microbe. Nor did the Black Death have the vile side effects of the Lenin pestilence of children betraying their parents, of relatives and friends accusing each other of the most fantastic crimes.

Lenin told those who complained about the terrible bloodshed caused by the revolution: "It does not matter if three-fourths of mankind perish! The only thing that matters is that, in the end, the remaining fourth should become Communist." He spoke nonchalantly of sacrificing three generations to bring about the electrification of Russia. His formula for an ideal Russia was justice plus electricity. The result so far has been no justice and little electricity.

Those of us born with the century know that unlucky countries have revolutions; lucky countries learn from other people's revolutions.

# The Trader's Role in History

## November 16, 1969

The truth that in human affairs the trivial is not trivial is nowhere more clearly demonstrated than in the vital role the trader played in history. Buying cheap and selling dear is admittedly a trivial and questionable activity. But, it is one of the few valid historical generalizations that every intense production of art, ideas, and spiritual values has occurred in some locality where a remarkable degree of trade activity was also taking place.

All through history the trader was quick to lodge himself in any cracks which appeared in the monolithic walls of totalitarian governments, and did all he could to widen them. And, as we watch the present goings on in the Communist world, where the black-marketeers are the only true revolutionaries, the realization is forced upon us that trading is a form of self-assertion congenial to common people—a sort of subversive activity, undoctrinaire, unheroic and uncoordinated, yet ceaselessly undermining and frustrating totalitarian domination.

It is true that in some instances in the past when the trader felt himself supreme he became as ruthless as any other ruling class. But on the whole, trade has been a catalyst of movement and change, and of government by persuasion rather than by coercion.

It was not a mere accident that the prophets, the Ionian philosophers[126], Confucius and Buddha made their appearance in a period in which traders were conspicuous and often dominant. The same was of course true of the birth of the Renaissance, and of the growth of science, literature, and art in modern times.

---

[126] Ionian school of Greek philosophy during the 6th and 5th centuries B.C.

# The Tragic Paradox of Our Cities

**November 23, 1969**

Our attitude toward nature implies a specific attitude not only toward man but also toward the city. The "wilderness boys" bristle with indignation when told that the city has been the seedbed of all human achievements. Most nature-worshippers see the manmade world of the city as artificial, stifling, and dehumanizing. They want to get close to nature, unite with it, and become "natural."

It is true that cities are built by nature-taming races. The city has been the general headquarters of the battle with nature.

Who ever heard of anything new conceived and invented in a village? Man's greatest achievements were conceived and realized not in the bracing atmosphere of mountains, plains, and forests, but in the crowded smelly cities of ancient Mesopotamia and Egypt, and in Jerusalem, Athens, Florence, Amsterdam, London, Paris and New York.

Men who live close to nature have little occasion to experience continuous progress toward something new and better. What impresses them rather is the recurrence of the old, the endless repetition of similar events. In the village there is a concern with security rather than adventure.

To develop his unique potentialities, man had to cut himself off from nature, and it was in the city that he cut himself off not only from the non-human cosmos but also from clans, tribes and other primitive modes of organization. Moreover, the city is a place where people of different bents and pursuits rub shoulders, where minds are cross-fertilized, and where is found the concentration of circumstances which prompts people to ask new questions, tinker with new possibilities and combine familiar elements into new compounds.

Thus for millennia man dotted the face of the earth with cities, his most fabulous invention.

The tragic paradox of our time is that just when our mastery over nature has reached unprecedented proportions, our cities are falling into decay. In the past, cities decayed because they lost the battle with nature and could no longer support themselves. Our cities are decaying at a moment when our victory over nature around us is almost total, and affluence is widely diffused.

We suddenly find ourselves battling nature in the cores of our affluent cities. It is inside our cities just now that nature is striking back at us, pushing us back into the jungle, and turning us into primitive savages.

# In Time of Rapid Change

November 30, 1969

What happens when things change so rapidly that the present shrinks to a mere hairline separating past from future?

The answer to this question is peculiar: When the present is almost nonexistent, future and past, too, become blurred. The future is so immediate that one no longer hopes and waits for it. Hope turns into desire. At the same time rapid change impairs memory. Yesterday seems distant, beyond recall.

It is a state of affairs ideally suited to the inclinations of the adolescent. He contemptuously dismisses the fact that he has no past, since the past is irrelevant. Nor can he see any sense in wasting his time preparing himself for the future. Tomorrow is now.

When skills and experience are made obsolete by drastic change, the dividing line between grownups and the young becomes blurred. Yet this is the time when the antagonism between generations is likely to be greatest. The young are arrogant in an age of not knowing, when the old no longer think themselves in possession of the true and only view possible for sensible people, and growing up becomes meaningless.

★

In an age of drastic change, even if it be an age of automation, nothing happens automatically. Everything has to be watched over and guarded; nothing can be taken for granted. When everything seems possible, the familiar becomes unpredictable. There are no established habits, customs, traditions, routines, and patterns—none of the arrangements which make everyday life self-starting and self-regulating.

Hence, unavoidably, an age of drastic change becomes an age of imposed regulation, and of regimentation. In other words, the vanishing of an established social automatism eventually leads to the conversion of autonomous individuals into automata.

It becomes evident, therefore, that if drastic change is to proceed in an orderly manner, without explosive byproducts, there is a vital need for the preservation of some continuity with the past. The changes have to take place within a preserved and reinforced framework.

Contrary to what the logicians tell us, drastic economic and social changes will proceed smoothly only if the political framework is left untouched, and if anything reinforced. The witches' brew of economic and social experimentation requires a sturdy, unbreakable political container.

# Man is Not One with Nature

## December 7, 1969

Man's ascent through the millennia must be seen as a cease-less striving to break away from the nonhuman cosmos. The age-long groping for freedom is an aspect of this blind striving to step outside the iron necessities which rule nature. The attempt to make human affairs as precise and predictable, as scientific, as a process in nature is an attempt at dehumanization.

The equation, human nature = nature, if read from left to right, gives us not only the scientific approach of Marx, Darwin, Freud and Pavlov but also the approach of ruthless soul engineers such as Lenin, Stalin, and Hitler who experimented with blood.

When read from right to left the equation gives us the magical approach, the belief that nature, not unlike human nature, can be influenced by words, and by other means which had proved their efficacy in the manipulation of human affairs.

Thus both the scientific and the magical approach postulate the oneness of man and nature, and both are agencies of dehu-manization. The Communists and the Nazis embraced both the scientific approach, of treating man as matter, and the magical approach, of trying to change reality by the power of words, by slogans and incantations.

In human affairs, all genuine opposites reflect the archetypal opposites of man and nature. Life and death, city and country, civilization and barbarism, free and slave, God and the devil, and perhaps even man and woman are such genuine opposites. On the other hand, oppressors and oppressed are not true opposites since both are dehumanized.

The same is true of the natural and the mechanical: Both are the opposite of that which is uniquely human. You dehumanize man as much by making him "natural" by making him one—with rocks, vegetables and animals, as by turning him into a machine. Nature, after all, is a perfectly, automated machine. To build something in the image of nature is to build a machine.

When you automate an industry you modernize it; when you automate a life you primitivize it. Man is God-like when he makes nature pliant and obedient, but he becomes an anti-God when he automates human beings and makes them pliant and obedient. For God turned malleable clay into man while anti-God turns man into malleable clay.

# The Nature of Civilization

December 14, 1969

Conditions optimal for a beginning are not necessarily favorable for continued growth and development. Africa, which had supposedly been the cradle of man, has not been a good milieu for human advance and the attainment of full humanization.

Civilization had its birth in Asia, yet in every case the civilizations of Asia had their growth arrested after a relatively short time, and if they did not crumble they continued in a state of stagnation for millennia.

In the Occident, so far, the situation has been the other way around. Europe could not create a civilization from scratch—it could not even invent a script of its own. Its civilization grew from a cutting brought from Asia. But once started, the civilization of Europe has shown an unprecedented capacity for continued growth and development.

The emergence of civilization was essentially a pulling away of the human species from the rest of creation. The cities which were the stage for the birth of civilization were enclaves cut off from nature, a manmade world wherein man could become uniquely human. Yet in Asia where cities were first born man's defenses against nature have remained precarious.

Again and again we find there nature bursting into the manmade enclaves and reclaiming what man has wrested from its grasp. You see trees cracking walls, heaving blocks of stone from their sockets and reclaiming once mighty cities. You have the feeling that in Asia the manmade world is precariously stretched over the writhing body of dragon nature.

Man in Asia has not had a sense of apartness from the predetermined inexorable and unalterable world of nature. In most Asiatic societies laws and customs had the implacability of laws of nature. Though the birth of civilization is hardly conceivable without the challenge of new questions, the civilizations of Asia once established functioned as if the answers were there before the questions.

For millennia in Asia men served as things, as raw material, and as means to an end. Outside the Western tradition the tendency has been to equate power with nature, and bow before tyranny as before a natural cataclysm.

Still, it was the penetration of the Orient into Europe through the vehicle of Christianity which created the ferment of creative vigor. The introduction of a religion of meekness and surrender among the warrior tribes of Europe created a polarity, a pull in opposite directions, which stretched souls. And it is the stretched soul only that makes music.

# Unnamed People Make History

December 21, 1969

It has been the fashion of historians for the past hundred years to belittle the role individuals play in shaping history. We are told that history is made by impersonal forces, by objective conditions, and by the blind necessity of inexorable laws.

A recent hefty book derives the nature of the various revolutions of our time from certain economic factors, particularly the relations between landlords and tenants, and this book does not have Lenin in its index.

Had Lenin been a microbe that caused the death of 50 million Russians no historian would dare ignore it as an historical factor, no matter how relevant the economic conditions. Since Lenin was a human being and not a microbe, he can be left unmentioned.

The amusing thing is that what intellectuals, including historians, want above all is to have a hand in the historic process. History-making is at present a disease of the self-appointed elite of the educated.

There is not a professor or a student who does not fancy himself qualified to tell the world what to do. The book of history lies open and every two-bit intellectual wants to turn its pages.

Now, to anyone who has lived through the first half of this century it is self-evident that history has been made by Lenin, Stalin, Hitler, Churchill, F.D.R., De Gaulle, Truman, Johnson and even Mussolini. What is not self-evident is the fact that history is also made by individuals who are not historical figures.

It would be difficult to exaggerate the degree to which anonymous examples triggered creative bursts or were the seed of new styles in the fields of action, thought, and imagination. Unremembered tinkerers first hit upon the cultivation of plants and the domestication of animals, and on the invention of the wheel, sail, brick making, etc.

Early in the 15th century, in the Netherlands, two brothers, Hubert[127] and Jan Van Eyck[128], started to paint magnificently with oil paints. How they got started is anybody's guess.

Mine is that some anonymous sign painter who was experimenting with oil paints happened to knock on the door of the Van Eyck household one wintry evening. He was taken in by the good housewife, given a bowl of hot lentil soup with dumplings, and something to drink.

Then, in an expansive, grateful mood the painter began to talk to the two boys who had been watching him intently. He talked volubly and enthusiastically about his new paints, showed how to prepare them, and let the boys handle his brushes. And so art history was written.

---

[127] Hurbert van Eyck (1385-1426), Flemish artist; among earliest oil painters.
[128] Jan van Eyck (1396-1441), Flemish artist; often and incorrectly attributed with inventing oil painting.

# Becoming Your Own Ancestor

### December 28, 1969

It cannot be repeated often enough: The only way Negroes can achieve power in this country is through organization. Organization is an accumulation of power without instruments of coercion. But organization is possible only among people who trust each other.

The chief task of Negro leadership is the creating and maintaining of mutual trust among Negroes. And my hunch is that such trust can come only through working together in some common undertaking.

Black cooperative undertakings, inside or outside the city, are more vital just now than black individual capitalism. Negroes should be induced to start common enterprises whether it be a building company, a machine shop or even a store. The strain of competition to which the Negro is not inured must be softened by cooperative striving.

Even when individual Negroes go into business on their own they ought to associate with their like in some mutual enterprise such as cooperative buying and mutual protection and insurance. The healing of the Negro's soul will come not from his integration with white people but from his integration with other Negroes.

It is also questionable whether Negro pride can be generated by individual success. No matter how manifest his superiority as an individual, the Negro in America cannot savor the unbought grace of life unless he can be proud of his people. He is a Negro first and only secondly an individual.

★

Any way you look at it, whether as a buffer against the strain of competition, or as a means of attaining power, or as a source of pride, the salvation of the Negro is in cooperative efforts.

Finally, it is doubtful whether the Negro can derive durable pride from an identification with a fictitious past of bogus empires in Ghana, Congo or Mali. The plain fact is that the Negro in America has to be his own ancestor. He has to make his own history. Fuzzy wuzzy hairdos, animal teeth necklaces, and Swahili patter cannot produce one atom of genuine pride.

Anyhow, in this country we are not interested in ancestors. It is preposterous that so much of the Negro's energies should go into self-dramatization and rhetoric. It is infinitely easier to rage, threaten, brag and posture than to build and create together.

# Inspired Luxuries

January 4, 1970

Man is a luxury-loving animal. His greatest exertions are made in pursuit not of necessities but of superfluities. Most of man's inventions, even those which seem designed for the satisfaction of simple needs, were originally conceived and employed in the obtaining of the extravagant and nonessential.

It is quite plausible that grain was first domesticated for the brewing of beer rather than for the making of bread. It is also safe to assume that man baked cake before he baked bread, just as he wore ornaments before he wore clothes. Temples and sepulchers are more ancient than plain houses. The first domesticated animals were pets.

★

The passionate pursuit of the nonessential and the extravagant is one of the chief traits of human uniqueness. Take away play, fancies and luxuries and you will turn man into a dull, sluggish creature, barely energetic enough to obtain a bare subsistence. It has been proven again and again that a population too sober and reasonable to exert itself in the pursuit of superfluities, becomes stagnant and ends up lacking in necessities. The people who set out to discover a new world were seeking not bread and shelter but gold and spices. It is well to remember that to artists and children luxuries are more essential than necessities.

In the Occident, the first machines were mechanical toys, and such crucial instruments as the telescope and the microscope were first conceived as playthings. Chloroform was used in parlor games before it was used in surgery. Gunpowder was invented to make firecrackers rather than bombs, and the bow was a musical instrument before it became a weapon.

★

The creative mind is the playful mind. Philosophy is the play and dance of ideas. Archimedes' bathtub and Newton's apple suggest that momentous trains of thought may have their inception in idle musing.

The original insight is most likely to come when elements stored in different compartments of the mind drift into the open, jostle one another, and now and then coalesce to form new combinations.

It is doubtful whether a mind that is pinned down and cannot drift elsewhere is capable of formulating new questions. The sudden illumination and the flash of discovery are not likely to materialize under pressure.

# The Dangers of Affluence

## January 11, 1970

In man's life, the lack of an essential component usually leads to the adoption of a substitute. The substitute is usually embraced with vehemence and extremism, for we have to convince ourselves that what we took as second choice is the best there ever was.

Thus blind faith is to a considerable extent a substitute for the lost faith in ourselves; insatiable desire is a substitute for hope; accumulation is a substitute for growth; fervent hustling a substitute for purposeful action, and pride a substitute for unattainable self-respect.

All through the millennia of his existence on this planet, man derived the ingredients of confidence, self-respect, hope, growth and purpose from strenuous striving and the overcoming of obstacles. Our values and standards are still reflecting the realities of scarcity, and struggle.

So long as these values continue to prevail it is questionable whether spectacular economic and social betterment could free us from our ills, and usher in an era of unprecedented peace and goodwill. Under our present scheme of values, affluence and leisure may generate tensions and strains which will threaten social dissolution.

In an indolent population living off the fat of the land the vital need for an unquestioned sense of worth and usefulness is bound to find expression in a hectic pursuit of explosive substitutes. The substitute of pride in particular is likely to become a source of divisiveness and strife.

The pride that at present pervades the world is the claim that one is a member of a chosen group—be it a nation, race, or party. No other attitude has so impaired the oneness of the human species, and contributed so much to the savage strife of our time.

If affluence is not to set in motion social dissolution we must change our conception of what is worthwhile, useful and efficient. Now that the new industrial revolution is on the way to solving the problem of means and we can catch our breath, it behooves us to remember that man's only legitimate end in life is to finish God's work—to bring to full growth the capacities and talents implanted in us.

A population dedicated to this end will not necessarily overflow with the milk of human kindness but it will not be likely to spend its time and energies proclaiming the superiority and exclusiveness of its nation, race, or doctrine.

# An Isolated Israel Survives

### January 18, 1970

There is no reason to assume that the people who shape America's foreign policy are naive enough to assume that by helping Nasser and other Arab loudmouths to get what they want most, namely the defeat of Israel, we would win over the Arab world to our side.

One need not be a prophet to predict that, no matter how pro-Arab our policy might be, an Arab victory would be accompanied by an hysterical defiance of America and the West. A triumphant Nasser would grab every oil field in the Middle East and would have the oil companies licking his boots. He would not only keep Arab ports closed to the Sixth Fleet, but might just for the heck of it to show who is who, deny American ships passage through the Suez Canal.

The simple truth is that it is in America's interest to keep things as they are. It is not in our interest to open the Suez Canal to Russian ships hauling cargo to North Vietnam. It is not in our interest to weaken Israel, our only trusted and battle-tested friend in the Mediterranean, or for that matter anywhere else.

A strong Israel will never involve us in a war. Israel does not ask for an American commitment for the simple reason that such a commitment would not be worth the paper it is written on. No country on this planet is going to fight for Israel. No country lifted a finger to save 8 million Jewish men, women and children from Hitler's gas chambers. No country showed the least inclination to come to Israel's aid in the spring of 1967 when Nasser blockaded the Gulf of Aqaba, mobilized umpteen divisions and hundreds of tanks in the north of the Sinai peninsula, and Jordanian and Syrian divisions in the east of Israel, and openly proclaimed his aim to wipe Israel off the map. Nor is there any reason to believe that the Sixth Fleet would lift a finger should Russian ships start to lob bombs into Israel.

America is not in the mood to get involved in a new war. Israel does not delude itself. It knows that it must fight alone.

To the Israelis the status quo is an acceptable solution to their problem.

The "Arab world" is a myth. The Arabs cannot strive and build, cannot fight, and cannot bide their time. All they can do is threaten, brag, lie and cry. A battalion of Israelis' could capture and hold the Arabian oil fields. An American air force based on the Sinai peninsula could more effectively checkmate the Russians than the Sixth Fleet.

Let us hope that the present pro-Arab noises in Washington are only moves in a diplomatic game. It fares ill with a country when its government is unable to recognize its enemies, or even prefers them to friends.

# The Influence of Things Yet to Be

## January 25, 1970

We are less ready to die for what we have or are, than for what we wish to have and to be. It is a perplexing and unpleasant truth that when men already have "something worth fighting for," they do not feel like fighting. Craving, not having, is the mother of a reckless giving of oneself.

"Things which are not" are indeed mightier than "things that are."

In all ages men fought most desperately for beautiful cities yet to be built and gardens yet to be planted. Satan did not digress to tell all he knew when he said: "All that a man hath will he give for his life." All he hath—yes. But he sooner dies than yield aught of that which he hath not yet.

It is indeed strange that those who hug the present and hang on to it with all their might should be the least capable of defending it. And that, on the other hand, those who spurn the present and dust their hands of it should have all its gifts and treasures showered on them unasked.

Dreams, visions and wild hopes are mighty weapons and realistic tools. The practical-mindedness of a true leader insists in recognizing the practical value of these tools. Yet, this recognition usually stems from a contempt of the present which can be traced to a natural ineptitude in practical affairs.

The successful businessman is often a failure as a communal leader because his mind is attuned to the "things that are" and his heart set on that which can be accomplished in "our time."

It is not altogether absurd that people should be ready to die for a button, a flag, a word, an opinion, a myth and so on. It is on the contrary the least reasonable thing to give one's life for something palpably worth having. For, surely, one's life is the most real of all things real, and without it there can be no having of things worth having.

Self-sacrifice cannot be a manifestation of tangible self-interest. Even when we are ready to die in order not to get killed, the impulse to fight springs less from self-interest than from intangibles such as tradition, honor and, above all, hope.

Where there is no hope, people either run, or allow themselves to be killed without a fight. The Jews who submitted to extermination in Hitler's Europe fought recklessly when transferred to Palestine.

And though it is said that they fought in Palestine because they had no choice—they had to fight or have their throats cut by the Arabs—it is still true that their daring and reckless readiness for self-sacrifice sprang not from despair but from their fervent preoccupation with the revival of an ancient land and an ancient people.

They, indeed, fought and died for cities yet to be built and gardens yet to be planted.

# Who Really Does the Work?

February 1, 1970

Not so long ago James Baldwin was running around Europe telling people what awful things would happen in America if Negroes stopped working. "America," he said, "would be paralyzed."

Now any child knows that if every Negro in America went on a strike some nightclubs and ball clubs might have to work short-handed, but if we should stop working, every Negro would starve.

An awful lot of Negroes are spending an awful lot of time figuring how many billions this country owes them. To my sort of people, who make up about 80% of the population, the idea that the country owes the Negro a doggoned thing sounds crazy.

The majority of us started to work for a living in our teens, and we have been poor much of our lives. Most of us had only a rudimentary education. Our white skin brought us no privileges and no favors.

The Negroes I worked with in the fields of California and on the San Francisco waterfront ate as well or better than I did, lived in as good or better houses, and many of them had more schooling.

Right now if my sort of people should wake up one morning and find that they have turned Negro overnight, their potential would increase tenfold.

A Negro who can read and write and is willing to apply himself has right now breathtaking prospects in this country. He can get into any college he chooses, get any number of scholarships, and have his pick of jobs when he graduates.

If he feels like it, he can cook up an autobiography telling the world about his miserable childhood, his nightmares, his rags, etc. etc., and any number of publishers will be fighting to buy it.

No Negro has ever done my work for me. If you pair up with a Negro on the waterfront, you consider yourself fortunate if your partner does his share. Has Negro work made the South rich?

The Black Power loudmouths are proclaiming from housetops that Negroes in America "are a colonized people in every sense of the term," that white America "is an organized imperialist force holding black people in colonial bondage."

This surely is a novel kind of colonialism where the colonialists are not a tiny minority but a vast majority, nine times the number of the colonialees, and in addition do all the hard work.

# A Workingman's Paradise

February 8, 1970

The fact sticks out: American businessmen, intellectuals, soldiers, technicians can work and live abroad; but not the American workingman! About the only place abroad where the American workingman might feel at home would be the communal settlements in Israel where there is neither pay nor bosses.

The chief reason that the American soldiers who defected to China during the Korean war returned home was that they could not fit in there as workingmen. Had they been intellectuals they would have probably stayed put. It is of interest that American gangsters, too, can never feel at home abroad.

There is the story about a British intellectual who traveled through this country toward the end of the last century. He was mortified by the monotony of the name of the towns he saw through the train window—Thomasville, Richardville, Harrysville, Marysville and so on. He had not an inkling of the import of what he saw. Namely that in this country, for the first time in history, common people—any Tom, Dick and Harry—could build a town and name it after himself or his wife.

At one station an old Irish woman got on the train and sat next to him. When she heard his muttering and hissing she said: "This is a blessed country, sir; I think God made it for the poor."

The common people everywhere have always looked on the United States as their country. You would not know this by reading foreign newspapers or by listening to foreign leaders and spokesmen. But the common people have voted for us with their legs by coming over to this country in their millions.

Right now my impression is that the organized workingman has it best in this country. People on top work longer hours, worry more, and probably die younger. Many of them make money while they sleep, but they do not sleep well.

The rich have it probably better elsewhere. Up to now in this country the rich did not know how to be at ease and how to savor their riches. Many of them did not know how to behave and came to a bad end. During the Renaissance the rich were in their element. They participated wholeheartedly in the political and cultural affairs of their cities. In the Old World the rich still seem to know how to enjoy their advantage.

People who lust for power are not likely to be happy in America. Here neither money nor education equips a man for the attainment of power. The opportunities in America are for learning, experience, money, achievement, comfort, freedom, but not for power.

# Rich and Righteous

February 15, 1970

It used to be taken for granted that the rich exploit the poor. But nowadays as you listen to the talk of some of the rich you get the impression that what they want most is to ally themselves with the poor against those of us in between. In the 1960s persons of great wealth have been a major source of support for radical political activity.

These rich idealists live in exclusive neighborhoods, send their children to exclusive schools and make use of every imaginable tax loophole, yet they view with anger and contempt the common folk who refuse to have their children bussed to outer darkness, who vote against compulsory integration of housing, and who do not tax themselves to the utmost to fight the evils which beset our cities.

In addition to a monopoly of wealth the new type of rich have a monopoly of righteousness. They savor the exquisite pleasure of being alienated on a hundred thousand a year.

Moreover, the radical rich have begotten radical sons. The rich men's sons of the SDS condemn the mass of people as racists and fascists because we do not elect Negroes for mayors, and because we side with the police who stand between us and this spreading reign of terror in the cities. The rich parents applaud and subsidize their revolutionary sons.

There is no generation gap. The misbegotten Mark Rudd[129] who called Dean Truman[130] of Columbia an obscene epithet in front of 200 faculty and students has a simpering ninny of a mother who dotes on him.

Would it be unjust to visit the sins of the sons on their parents? Why should not these tax-dodging parents of draft-dodging sons be sued for damage done to property, for foul-mouthed insults heaped on university officials, and for interfering with the education of less favored students?

---

[129] Mark Rudd (1947- ), American political organizer involved with the Weather Underground—a violent, radical left organization.
[130] David Bicknell Truman (1913-2003), American academic involved in the 1968 Columbia University student protests.

# Is a Revolution Revolutionary?

## March 1, 1970

One of the startling discoveries of our times is that non-revolutionary countries are far more revolutionary than revolutionary countries. We have been slow to realize that revolutions are actually anti-revolutionary—that they lead not to a wholly new future but back to a distant past.

During the last several decades the most startling changes have taken place in free countries. Think of what has happen in this country. In less than two decades we have been transported to a new age, and to almost a new country. The days of 1950 seem far off and semi-mythical.

The so-called revolutionary countries are stuck in the mud. Present-day Russia is still Russia of the czars and khans. It is still locked in the problems of its dark past. A Communist revolution is everywhere a return to feudal times when the soil and the tillers of the soil were the property of the state. When a Communist country Czechoslovakia tried to shake itself out of its torpor it became self-evident that it had to join the free non-revolutionary world.

It is now a truism that countries are transformed more dramatically by Americanization than by a Communist revolution.

Incredible psychological changes have occurred in non-revolutionary countries. The warlike Japanese and Germans have become the world's foremost traders, and the Jews the foremost warriors. Hereditary enemies like Germany and France have become close collaborators.

A united Europe is becoming an attainable goal. Poor countries like Saudi Arabia and Libya have become fabulously rich overnight. The free world is a seething alembic in which nations are transmuted and new entities synthesized

It is conceivable that if the rate of change in the free world accelerates beyond human endurance we might need some sort of revolution to slow it down.

One reason for the lethargy of revolutionary countries is their perpetuation of scarcity. Diffused affluence is becoming the monopoly of free countries, and we are discovering that affluence is a more potent source of upheaval than poverty.

Diffused affluence deprives riches of its uniqueness, robs the rich of a sense of fulfillment, and makes poverty seem a disease that demands an instant cure. Thus in an affluent society both the rich and the poor are hospitable to change.

# Reflections on a Minority Revolution

## March 15, 1970

It is questionable whether the Negro Revolution will have a fateful effect on the Negro. The Negro's future in this country will depend on his ability to compete and excel, and on his capacity for patient, hard work. If the Negro cannot learn to strive and build on his own he will remain lowest on the totem pole no matter how loud and explosive his slogans, and how extravagant his self-dramatization.

Nevertheless, the Negro Revolution is a fateful event—not because of what it is doing to the Negro, but because of its effects on segments of the non-Negro population.

The effect of the Negro Revolution on the non-Negro young is as unexpected as it is puzzling. Why have the young so whole-heartedly adopted the Negro's style of life? The negrification of the young will have profound and durable effects on our language, sexual mores, the attitude toward work, and on tastes and manners in general. Even young white racists are negrified and do not realize it.

Equally fateful is the effect of the Negro Revolution on ethnic groups. Not only have Puerto Ricans, Mexicans and Indians been emboldened to adopt the Negro tactics, but the entrance of the Negro into the mainstream of American life is bringing about a reversion of amalgamation in the melting pot.

Everywhere you look you see some degree of ethnic crystallization. The fact that the WASP uppercrust has shown a tendency to conciliate Negro militants at the expense of those in the middle has caused the ethical to lose faith in the Mayflower boys. More and more they are beginning to vote for candidates of their own group.

The Negro Revolution has also brought the policeman onto the political stage. Policemen are getting elected mayors of large cities and if Negro lawlessness continues and escalates we may have policeman elected president. Middle income Americans who do most of the work, pay much of the taxes and do most of the voting are convinced that order comes first—that without order there can be no justice, no freedom and no civilized living.

Finally, the Negro Revolution is transplanting the South to the big cities, and there is a chance that the South will break out of its political isolation. The pressed, worried and silent white males of large cities may find their spokesmen in articulate Southern politicians who will rid themselves of Confederate impediments and play the role of genuine national representatives.

# Reflections on Mankind

April 5, 1970

Man is the only young thing in the world. A deadly seriousness emanates from all other forms of life. The cry of pain and of fear man has in common with other living things, but he alone can smile and laugh.

Man's thoughts and imaginings are the music drawn from the taut strings of the soul. The stretching of the soul that produces music is the result of a pull of opposites—opposite bents, attachments, yearnings. Where there is no polarity—where energies flow smoothly in one direction—there can be hustle and noise but no music.

That which is unique and worthwhile in us makes itself felt only in flashes. If we do not know how to catch and savor these flashes, we are without growth and without exhilaration.

They who lack talent expect things to happen without effort. They ascribe failure to a lack of inspiration or of ability, or to misfortune, rather than to insufficient application. At the core of every true talent there is an awareness of the difficulties inherent in any achievement, and the confidence that by persistence and patience something worthwhile will be realized. Thus, talent is a species of vigor.

The remarkable thing is that it is the crowded life that is most easily remembered. A life full of turns, achievements, disappointments, surprises, and crises is a life full of landmarks. The empty life has even its few details blurred and cannot be remembered with certainty.

Sensuality reconciles us with the human race. The misanthropy of the old is due in large part to the fading of the magic glow of desire.

When we begin to think that most people are no better than we, the world seems full of people who are fairly unpleasant.

There is probably an element of malice in our readiness to overestimate people—we are, as it were, laying up for ourselves the pleasure of later cutting them down to size.

It is a sign of creeping inner death when we no longer can praise the living.

In human affairs every solution serves only to sharpen the problem, to show us more clearly what we are up against. There are no final solutions.

# Man's Ascent from Playful Savagery

## April 12, 1970

Man learned to paint, carve, sculpt, and model in clay long before he made a pot or wove cloth or domesticated an animal. Man as an artist is infinitely more ancient than man as a worker.

The prevailing opinion seems to be that man's ascent through the millennia has been a grim affair. We picture to ourselves the life of earliest man as unimaginably hard and dangerous, a violent and protracted duel, always facing the problem of how to eat without being eaten, never knowing, on retiring, whether he would be there in the morning. Yet as we trace back the aptitudes, skills, and practices which enabled man to survive and gain mastery over his environment, we always reach the realm of play.

Most utilitarian devices and inventions had their birth in non-utilitarian pursuits. The first domesticated animal—the dog puppy—was not the most useful but the most playful animal. Man's inventiveness and his flashes of insight come not when he is grubbing for necessities, but when he reaches out, for the superfluous and the extravagant. Play is older than work, art older than production for use. Man was shaped less by what he had to do than by what he did in playful moments.

Hence it is reasonable to assume that the humanization of man occurred in surroundings where nature was bountiful and man did not have to fight her tooth and nail. The ascent of man was enacted in something like an Eden playground rather than on a desolate battlefield.

★

235

The contemporary explosion of avant-garde innovation in literature, art, and music is wholly unprecedented. The nearest thing that comes to mind is the outburst of sectarian innovation at the time of the Reformation, when every yokel felt competent to start a new religion.

What is there at present in the cultural sphere which corresponds to the shattering of an authoritarian church in the 16th century?

Obviously what our age has in common with the age of the Reformation is the fallout of disintegrating values. What needs explaining is the presence of a receptive audience. More significant than the fact that poets write abstrusely, painters paint abstractly, and composers compose unintelligible music is that people should admire what they cannot understand; admire that which has no meaning on principle.

# Reflections on America

April 19, 1970

People who lust for power are not likely to be happy in America. Here neither money nor education equip a man for the attainment of power. The opportunities in America are for learning, experience, money, achievement, comfort, freedom, but not for power.

One of the chief problems a modern society has to face is how to provide an outlet for the intellectual's restless energies yet deny him power. How to make and keep him a paper tiger.

The intellectual will feel at home where an exclusive elite is in charge of affairs, and it matters not whether it be an elite of aristocrats, soldiers, merchants or intellectuals. He would prefer an elite that is culturally literate, but will put up with one that is not. What he cannot endure is a society dominated by common people. There is nothing he loathes more than government of and by the people.

It is doubtful whether the oppressed ever fight for freedom. They fight for pride and for power—power to oppress others. The oppressed want above all to imitate their oppressor; they want to retaliate.

Both the revolutionary and the creative individual are perpetual juveniles. The revolutionary does not grow up because he cannot grow, while the creative individual cannot grow up because he keeps growing.

It seems that the most important revolutions are those other people make for us. The French Revolution altered France relatively little, but it created Germany. Similarly, the fateful consequences of the Russian Revolution will be a United Europe and a

237

new China. The revolutionary nature of the Negro Revolution will manifest itself more in its effects on the white students and juveniles than in a transformation of the Negro's existence.

The American is much better than his words. In other civilizations it is legitimate to assume that what people profess is on a higher level than what they practice. With the mass of people in America it is the other way around: Their acts are more sensitive and original than their professed opinions. They practice, as it were, an inverted hypocrisy.

It is too late in the day for Americans to try to win anyone with words, and it is even more certain that we cannot win by giving. What then can we do? We can win the world only by example—by making our way of life as good as we know how. Our main problem is not the world but ourselves, and we can win the world only by overcoming ourselves.

# Lonely on the Face of the Earth

## April 26, 1970

To feel wholly at home in this world is to partake of the nature of plants and animals. Man is an eternal stranger in this world. He became a stranger when he cut himself off from the rest of creation and became human. From this incurable strangeness stems our incurable uncertainty, our unfulfillable craving for roots, our passion to cover the world with manmade compounds, our need for a God who appoints us as His viceroy on earth.

The God who created nature was above all a supreme technician. But once He had created nature and automated it, God lost interest in His creation. It bored Him, and in His boredom God became an artist, and He created man in His own image—the image of an artist.

All other animals are perfect technicians, each with its built-in toolkit, each an accomplished specialist. Man is a technically misbegotten creature, half finished and ill equipped, but in his mind and soul are all the ingredients of a creator, of an artist. And it was God's mark as a supreme artist that He refused to automate man.

When trying to determine the role Christianity played in the rise of the modern Occident, it is necessary to remember that it was a weakening of the Christian faith that marked the birth of our present civilization. The loss of religious faith was probably more decisive than any peculiarly Christian doctrine or attribute. Most often when we renounce a faith, we do not cast it off, but swallow it: We substitute the self for the abandoned holy cause. Hence the weakening of an ardent faith may result not in lethargy but in an

239

intensification of the individual's drive. What is decisive is not that we are without a religious faith, but that we had a god and lost faith in him. It is this rejection and usurpation of a once ardently worshiped god which has had fateful effects on society and the individual in the modern Occident.

It is startling to realize that between 1400 and 1800 A.D. the Eastern influence on the West was far greater than the Western influence on the East. Were it not for the Eastern influence, Columbus might not have set out to discover America. It is well to remember that Asia gave us the instruments—gunpowder, the compass, the astrolabe—with which to subdue it.

# Index

Former migratory worker and longshoreman, Eric Hoffer burst on the scene in 1951 with his irreplaceable tome, *The True Believer*, and assured his place among the most important thinkers of the twentieth century. Nine books later, Hoffer remains a vital figure with his cogent insights to the nature of mass movements and the essence of humankind.

Of his early life, Hoffer has written: "I had no schooling. I was practically

Hoffer in the old San Francisco Public Library

blind up to the age of fifteen. When my eyesight came back, I was seized with an enormous hunger for the printed word. I read indiscriminately everything within reach—English and German.

"When my father (a cabinetmaker) died, I realized that I would have to fend for myself. I knew several things: One, that I didn't want to work in a factory; two, that I couldn't stand being dependent on the good graces of a boss; three, that I was going to stay poor; four, that I had to get out of New York. Logic told me that California was the poor man's country."

Through ten years as a migratory worker and as a gold-miner around Nevada City, Hoffer labored hard but continued to read and write during the years of the Great Depression. The Okies and the Arkies were the "new pioneers," and Hoffer was one of them. He had library cards in a dozen towns along the railroad, and when he could afford it, he took a room near a library for concentrated thinking and writing.

In 1943, Hoffer chose the longshoreman's life and settled in California. Eventually, he worked three days each week and spent one day as "research professor" at the University of California in Berkeley. In 1964, he was the subject of twelve half-hour programs on national television. He was awarded the Presidential Medal of Freedom in 1983.

CPSIA information can be obtained
at www.ICGtesting.com
Printed in the USA
LVHW091023140419
614124LV00002B/398/P

9 781933 435374